# CHAKRAS AND THEIR ARCHETYPES

# CHAKRAS AND THEIR ARCHETYPES

## Uniting Energy Awareness and Spiritual Growth

### AMBIKA WAUTERS

CROSSING PRESS
Berkeley

Published in the United States by Crossing Press, an imprint of the Crown
Publishing Group, a division of Random House, Inc., New York.
www.crownpublishing.com
www.tenspeed.com

Crossing Press and the Crossing Press colophon are registered trademarks of
Random House, Inc.

First published in 1996 by Judy Piatkus (Publishers) Ltd in London


**Library of Congress Cataloging-in-Publication Data**

Wauters, Ambika.
    [Journey of self discovery]
    Chakras and their archetypes : uniting energy awareness and spiritual growth / Ambika Wauters.
        p.   cm.
    Originally published; Journey of self discovery. U.K. : J. Piatkus, 1989.
    Includes bibliographical references.


    1. Chakras—Miscellanea.  2. Archetype (Psychology)—Miscellanea.  I. Title.
BF1442.C53W39   1997
   158.1—dc21                                   97-25539
                                                            CIP
ISBN-13: 978-0-89594-891-5


Printed in the United States of America
Cover design by Victoria May, based on artwork by Carol Jones and Ken Leeder

20 19 18 17 16 15 14
First U.S. Edition

*This book is dedicated to Inelia Ahumada Avila*
*who lived and died with grace and dignity.*
*She was a delight to us all.*

---

I would like to thank the people who cared about and supported me while I was writing this book. At each stage of transformation I lived through each archetype and experienced its energy in my life. Some good friends stayed throughout the whole process while others departed from my life.

My love goes to Sandy Cotter, Andy Logan, Mary Jardine, Chrissy Pickin, Josh Enkin, Sue Bell, Anne Carter, Stephanie Barraclough and Allison Jackson-Bass. Your friendship means so much to me and I am grateful to you all for the love and support you unequivocally offer me. My gratitude also goes to my homoeopathic teachers and mentors who, over the past six years of my training, have helped me to develop into a skilful practitioner. Thanks and love to Jude Creswell for guidance, direction and friendship and to Ian Townsend, Azizza Griffin, Bob Fordham and Gill Scott at the School of Homoeopathic Medicine (Darlington) who always offered superb teaching and were wonderful examples of real wisdom and true integrity. I am deeply grateful for the life tool of homoeopathy.

Thanks to Anthea Courtenay for her input and work on the text, Gill Cormode and Anne Lawrance at Piatkus for seeing it through, and, as always, my agent Susan Mears for her support.

Thanks too to Timothy Freke and Martin Palmer for permission to reproduce an extract from their edition of *Lao Tzu's Tao Te Ching* (Piatkus, 1995).

Gratitude to the teachers, clients and friends whose life stories have been inspiring. You showed me how transformation could qualitatively take place. I acknowledge and honor that spirit in us all.

Give up, and you will succeed.
Bow, and you will stand tall.
Be empty, and you will be filled.
Let go of the old, and let in the new.
Have little, and there is room to receive more.

The wise stand out,
because they see themselves as part of the Whole.
They shine,
because they don't want to impress.
They achieve great things,
because they don't look for recognition.
Their wisdom is contained in what they are,
not their opinions.
They refuse to argue,
so no one argues with them.

The Ancients said: "Give up and you will succeed."
Is this empty nonsense?
Try it.
If you are sincere, you will find fulfillment.

*Lao Tzu's Tao Te Ching,* Chapter 22
(Piatkus, 1995)

# CONTENTS

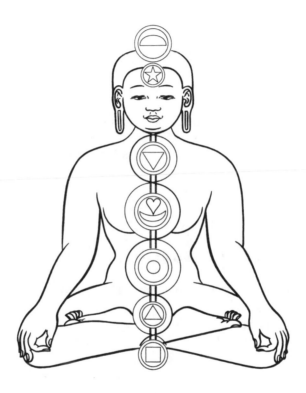

*The symbols on this Buddha show where the chakras are located.
In ascending order they are Root; Sacral; Solar Plexus; Heart;
Throat; Brow; and Crown.*

# INTRODUCTION

We all have a wish to mature into healthy and whole beings, and today many people are also seeking ways of developing their spiritual nature. Our culture makes it difficult for us to learn how to grow up emotionally and spiritually, and many of us are attempting to redress this imbalance through growth and development workshops, therapy sessions and personal experiences which teach us to value and empower ourselves by taking responsibility for our lives.

As a therapist and healer, I have frequently used the archetypes as a model for self-awareness and as a ladder towards spiritual growth. Since first reading Jung's *Archetypes of the Collective Unconscious* over 25 years ago, I have been amazed at how much insight I have gained about myself and my clients from focusing on the archetypes which emerge during our journey towards wholeness.

This book describes the relationship between the archetypes and the chakras, the seven main centers of the human energy system (see opposite). Connecting the archetypes with the chakras is a new concept which has come out of attempting to unite energy awareness with spiritual growth. In my workshops and in individual sessions I witness the effects of this work time and time again, as people develop and grow into whole and integrated individuals. In this book I am offering readers a guide to

freeing themselves of limiting, negative patterns which sap their vitality, and helping them to move towards greater freedom and empowerment.

# WHAT ARE ARCHETYPES?

Archetypes have emerged out of the core of human experience, and represent the
positive and the negative qualities within each of us. Every archetype represents a
particular, fixed pattern of human behavior; typical are the deities of ancient Greece
and Rome, the gods and goddesses of war, love, healing, communication and so on,
who are archetypes.

Archetypes are embodied in the characters which appear in myth and folklore
throughout the ages—the Beautiful Princess, the Wicked Witch, the Knight in Shining
Armor, and many more. They are also the projections of glamour and excitement we
see today in films and on television. The image of Marilyn Monroe, for example, is
a form of archetypal beauty and sexuality which represents the archetype of the Vamp
or Siren.

We respond to archetypes because they mirror aspects of our own unconscious.
Thus, when an archetypal character—whether hero or villain, wicked stepmother or
orphaned child—is portrayed in a film or play, we are struck by the deep emotional
response that character evokes and something within us resonates with them.

Archetypes emerge as the heroes and villains of every culture. The Warrior archetype has been represented by David in the Old Testament, by Achilles and Odysseus
in Greek mythology, and King Arthur in stories of the Round Table. He appears in all
the myths and stories which tell of the Hero's quest. The quintessential macho archetype of our own times is Rambo. The reason we enjoy these stories so much is that
they hold the appeal of the Warrior archetype who triumphs over tremendous odds.
We can all relate to this, since this plays a part in our own life's journey.

Archetypes are universal. The Mother archetype, for instance, has existed
throughout history in various guises and is valued in every culture. She represents
the feminine principle of creation, whether she is called Maria, Isis, Ishtar, Quan Yin
or Sophia. She is the spirit of love, purity and gentleness which lives within us all.

# ARCHETYPES AS A MIRROR

Archetypes are, in a sense, universal projections or mirrors of all the emotional qualities which come from the core of human experience—strength and weakness, love and hate, courage and fear. They show us our front and our back, our light and our shadow, our positive and our negative qualities. They represent, in essence, the multifaceted soul of human consciousness—the Hero and the Villain, the Fool and the Wise Man or Woman, the Giver and the Taker, the Destroyer and the Healer.

Our daily experiences in the world reflect the archetypes we are constellating in our inner emotional worlds; recognizing this can help us to understand our motivations and behavior more clearly. For instance, when we feel helpless in the face of difficult situations, we may be identified with the archetype of the Victim. But we can also recognize that we contain other, more positive archetypes like the Mother, the Warrior or the Wise Person. Whether we are male or female, these archetypal qualities exist within all of us, both as an ideal and as a potential to be expressed in our own lives. We can embody these qualities by loving and nourishing ourselves— in other words, by becoming our own Mother, Warrior or Wise Person archetype. Creating healthy archetypes in our lives is fundamental to our healing and growth.

When we upgrade our archetypes in this way, we have the opportunity to contact higher centers of awareness and to live from the deep wisdom within ourselves. In order for us to grow, the energy of any dysfunctional or negative archetype must be released so that we can free up the vital energy it is blocking. We need this energy now to get on with our lives and make them flourish.

# JUNG'S VIEW OF ARCHETYPES

In his book *Archetypes of the Collective Unconscious*, the psychoanalyst Carl Jung systematically revealed the existence of archetypes, which he defined as "patterns of behavior". According to Jung they are an essential part of our awareness which, if we allow them, can illuminate our unconscious ways of behaving, and help us in our task of enlightening the unconscious and the darker aspects of our personalities that Jung called the Shadow—those parts of us that have remained undeveloped because they have not been given expression.

I first read Jung's book when I was a young art student, over 25 years ago. It stimulated me to seek further information about archetypes and eventually to spend time at the Jung Institute in Zurich, Switzerland, studying them and the various ways they manifest in art, folklore, psychology and the occult sciences. My studies included the aboriginal people of Australia, who go into their "Dream Time" to make their connection with the higher spiritual archetypes of their culture, their Wise Men. I also studied the Tarot with a professor of clinical psychiatry who showed me the archetypal models found in the 21 cards of the Major Arcana, which represent stages in the journey of the soul.

While in Zurich, I was inspired by meeting the elderly men and women who had worked and studied together with Jung and his wife. They showed me what conscious and aware people could be like as a result of looking within themselves and weeding out negativity from their lives. Many of them were, by then, in their eighties; they were lively and alert and able to lecture without notes for hours. They transformed my ideas about ageing, and helped plant the seed for a new archetype for my senior years which could embody wisdom, grace and beauty. Ever since then, I have worked with the different archetypes to aid me in my personal growth, and facilitate my work as a healer, therapist and homoeopath.

It was Jung's theories which first encouraged me to consider archetypes as a way of recognizing aspects of myself I had not consciously experienced before. This helped me gather the courage to face my inner Shadow of unresolved conflicts and to bring light to the areas of my life which had previously been unexpressed.

## MY PERSONAL JOURNEY

My own youth was geared, like that of most young people in the 1960s, to trying to get it right to please my parents. I grew up in a middle-class Jewish family in which it was expected that I would get an education, marry and have children, with little encouragement to find a meaningful path for my life. Emotions were seldom expressed until my parents reached boiling point, when everything then spilled over on to the children. As a result, I spent years in therapy in an effort to release my deep frustration and feelings of unworthiness. The archetypal patterns of Victim, Martyr and Servant were part of the feminine archetypes in my family, and were imprinted in my subconscious mind from an early age.

In my twenties I was well married, according to my parents' wishes, but my life started to fall apart when I found I was unable to have children. This threw me directly into the Victim archetype. However, it was also opportunity disguised as loss—a recurring theme in my life—for it led me to seek the help of therapy, growth and transformation work.

My mother's death when I was 26 freed me to find out who I really was. My energy had been safely channeled into art, and soon afterwards I left my marriage and went to live in a therapeutic community in southern Spain, which offered three-month courses for people wishing to explore their inner nature. Here my gifts as a sensitive and healer first emerged, with the care and guidance of some excellent teachers and friends.

From there I went to study for a time at the Jung Institute, and then returned to the community in Spain as a staff member. I supported myself by giving art lessons to children, and making and selling things on the local gypsy market. It was an exciting time. I delved into the world of yoga, healing, meditation, bioenergetics and Gestalt therapy, macrobiotic cooking, and the wonderful company of like-minded people from all over the world who gathered at this center for learning and growth.

I felt ten years younger and very happy as I started to let go of the rigid archetypal patterns which had seriously limited my health, creativity and emotional expression. I began to live my life from the heart, rather than from time-worn ideas about how a nice Jewish girl should be. I was beginning to do what felt right for me, rather than what others thought I should be doing. In other words, my archetypes were shifting from those of Victim and Martyr to those of a more empowered woman. It was the beginning of real growth.

I went on to work as a bioenergetic therapist throughout Europe and the US, taking time off when I remarried and went to live in Zaire, in Africa. After ten years the gift of healing emerged again very strongly, and I had no choice but to pursue it. I came to England where I retrained as a homoeopath. This gave me more empowerment and satisfaction than anything I had done hitherto. As new archetypes emerged in my life, higher levels of learning came to me.

Over this long period of time, I have shifted from the Victim archetype to those of Mother, Martyr, Empress, Servant and Warrior, to find the path of the heart, the place of my Higher Self. I have had the help of some wonderful healers, therapists and spiritual friends. Each time I shifted archetypes, I found new teachers. I know that anyone making this journey is never alone. We are all guided and befriended on this path. Many people reached out and opened doors for me.

It has become increasingly easy to release those old, worn-out patterns of feeling that life is abusing me. I am able to contact my deep center and trust that the good is coming to me and that all will be well. The strength of my higher archetypes invariably serves my consciousness and facilitates my growth. I now acknowledge my needs and accept my feelings rather than blaming others. I feel I am creating the good and joyful things in my life.

My self-empowerment has taken many years; there were turns in the road that were sometimes frightening and lonely, but the insight and growth that came from taking risks, and knowing myself better, helped release my negativity and were always worth it. What emerged from all this was learning to trust my Higher Self and honor my spirit. I came to know that I was truly guided and protected by the Source within me. Each step of the way has helped me to define my purpose as a healer and put me in touch with myself. I also know that there is still more opening and healing as I walk down my path.

# ARCHETYPES AND ENERGY

The archetypes that we live out reflect the psychological patterning of self-care and worthiness, demonstrating the degree to which we love and cherish ourselves. They are a clear manifestation of our emotional state and the stage we have reached in our growth and maturation. These archetypes are also the metaphor for the strength of our vital energy, and the degree of creativity and pleasure we enjoy.

Highly empowered people have a vast amount of energy. They can work hard, have many interests and still have energy left over. On the other hand, people who are not empowered have little vital energy for themselves or for their pleasure; they are often ill and require a lot of attention. Much of their outlook is based on sacrifice and struggle, whether they have learned this as children or chosen it in adulthood.

It is this connection between the archetypes and energy that I have set out to explore in this book. As you work through it, you will see the direct link between the levels of personal responsibility, and the levels of energy and empowerment each archetype possesses. They represent a kind of ladder we all need to follow.

By making these connections within yourself you can use the archetypes as stepping stones towards developing higher states of consciousness. The more willing you are to take responsibility for your life, the more developed your archetype will become, and the more empowered and energetic you will be.

# ARCHETYPES AND THE CHAKRAS

There are many archetypes, just as there are many types of character. In this book I am concentrating on those that have particular relevance to the energetic dynamics of the chakras, or energy centers, in the human energy system. The chakras relate to archetypes in that both represent a measure of our emotional states, and both tell a story of our happiness, health, well-being and ability to love.

There are seven main chakras in the human energy system, and I will discuss them in greater detail in Chapter 2. They are points or vortices at which energy is filtered through our system; they help our energy to flow freely so that we can fulfill the task of living and express our maximum potential as creative beings. Each chakra relates, among other things, to a particular emotional state of being.

Over the course of my work, I became aware of a strong connection between the chakras and the archetypal roles that people play out in their lives. From the vast pool of archetypal characters I have chosen 14 which resonate with the emotional issues and vibrational frequencies found in the chakras. Each archetype is presented in both its positive and negative (or functional and dysfunctional) aspect, so that you can work with both. The relationships can be seen in the table on the next page.

# WORKING WITH THE ARCHETYPES

In this book we will be making a journey through the chakras and their related archetypes, each representing a stage in our spiritual growth. By recognizing these stages, in both their positive and negative aspects, you can work through them and move on to the next stage.

Each chapter introduces a specific chakra, and examines the negative and positive archetypes associated with it. In addition, each aspect of the archetype is represented in two case studies, one male and one female. These cases are an amalgamation of various people I have treated in my work, and they serve to illustrate the kinds of situation people face as they live out their archetypes, and how they can work with the archetypes to resolve their problems and become more empowered. These are followed by exercises, meditations and affirmations to help you release old patterns and fears, and focus your intention about what you want in life.

Doing this inner work will give you the opportunity to heal and grow; I have watched many people transform their lives through using the archetypes in this way. It can help to identify where you are stuck in your development, and, as you open up energy in the chakras and transform your archetypes, you will begin to move on and empower yourself.

| CHAKRA | ARCHETYPE | | EMOTIONAL ISSUES |
| --- | --- | --- | --- |
| | Positive | Negative | |
| Base | Mother | Victim | The ground of being |
| Sacral | Emperor/Empress | Martyr | Pleasure and well-being |
| Solar Plexus | Warrior | Servant | Power and self-worth |
| Heart | Lover | Actor | Love |
| Throat | Communicator | Silent Child | Effective communication |
| Brow | Intuitive | Intellectual | Use of information for happiness and health |
| Crown | Guru | Egotist | Highest spiritual awareness |

# 1

# ARCHETYPES AND THE MYTHS WE LIVE BY

## ARCHETYPES AS MODELS OF PERSONAL WHOLENESS

Archetypes are a universal projection of the collective thoughts and emotions of humanity, commonly called the collective unconscious. They provide us with models of what we are, and what we hope to become. In our own times, fictional characters and celebrities represent various aspects of our consciousness, and also teach us about our own inner qualities by showing us the scope of the human condition. In addition, life itself offers us the opportunity to see our own archetypes played out, acting as a mirror for our inner state and showing us stepping stones by which we can move forward on our path of self-development.

When we study myths and folklore it becomes clear that humanity has always embraced an ideal of personal wholeness. Ancient myths and modern films like *Braveheart* (1995) tell of the hero overcoming a series of ordeals in his search for spiritual and emotional wholeness, whether in the form of a hidden treasure or an enchanted princess. Often these seekers are offered special knowledge or help by a Wise Old Man or Woman, a Mage or an Old Crone.

We enjoy these tales of triumph, success and especially love; they teach us about the treasures of life, and can offer us the wisdom we need to value the real jewels of our personal experience. Their implicit message is that we must take risks, or lose our edge on life. The process of stepping forward in life is necessary to the continual journey which opens up our awareness and sense of discovery, giving us new truths and deeper insights.

## MYTHS AND CULTURE

In ancient times archetypes found their way first into oral story-telling and then into recorded myth. The archetypal images mirrored in these stories revealed the special qualities people needed to flourish in their culture, such as fighting prowess and cunning. Odysseus, for example, represents the Warrior archetype of his day, who has to use all his wits and cunning through his travels and adventures. Such myths become incorporated into the culture as ways of teaching people about wisdom and virtue, as well as examples of meeting life's challenges.

Stories and myths also reveal the level of a society's development. As societies evolved, so did the archetypal themes of their stories. In medieval literature, for instance, grace and justice were a theme of the legends of King Arthur and his knights. Tales like Perceval's quest for the Holy Grail (an archetype of the self) reflect the high spiritual values that were held in esteem at that time, while the Round Table stands for an archetype of wholeness.

Fairy tales, too, have value for a culture because they teach people, particularly the young, about qualities such as devotion, virtue and courage. For example, in the story of Cinderella we see the downtrodden youngest child of a dysfunctional family whose beauty is not allowed to shine, and who is abused and manipulated by her stepmother and jealous sisters. Cinderella is the archetypal Lover—pure of heart and innocent. Her mother is dead, and her father has failed to save her from the cruelty of his second wife.

The father represents the negative aspect of the Warrior archetype (the Servant), since he lacks the courage to stand up for what he knows is wrong, while the stepsisters embody the negative qualities of envy, greed and hatred. The fairy godmother is the archetypal Magician, who transforms simple, everyday objects into magical props to help Cinderella fulfil her destiny by meeting the prince.

We are reminded throughout this story of the archetypes of good and evil, and the role which destiny plays in our lives. We gain insight, even as children, into the corrosive quality of jealousy and rivalry, and learn how beauty and love can prevail over the darker aspects of the human spirit.

# LEARNING ABOUT OURSELVES THROUGH STORIES AND MYTHS

We can learn about ourselves by remembering which myths and stories we cherished as children. They showed us what was honored in our homes and communities, and those that fired our imagination and touched us deeply often remain imprinted on our minds. How many people still secretly long to find the beautiful princess, or to be rescued by a knight in shining armor?

You may find it useful to know which myths have influenced your life. If stories were part of your childhood, think about those you enjoyed, and what you may have incorporated from them into your belief system. Did you suffer with the orphan child in *The Little Match Girl* and identify with her? Or did you rally to *The Count of Monte Cristo*, believing that life could be a wonderful adventure in which you would always come through, no matter how difficult the situation?

We also assimilate the impressions we receive from fashion, films and music, and as we integrate their messages we make their ideals part of our lives as well as our own individual myth. Since we write the scripts of our own dramas, it is important to know at which level we wish to participate. Do we want to star as the Victim, the Hero or the Guru of our own life script? Into which roles do we project our thoughts and desires? How brightly do we want our star to shine?

It is valuable to be aware of these scripts, for they may not be serving us. It was only recently that I had the courage to look at my late mother's unhappiness and boredom, and realize how unfulfilled she was. Her archetype was the Martyr, and her myth was clearly about the princess who could never find happiness. No matter what she had, it was never quite good enough, but so long as she remained a Martyr she could never find the happiness she so desperately wanted.

I was expected to live out the myth that the women in my family had lived out for generations. As the oldest daughter of the oldest daughter, it was my role to make everyone happy and get things right for my family. To say the least, this myth did not last for too long. No one can try to live out someone else's fantasy and expect to be happy. But it took a lot of time, and real work on myself, before I could start living from that place in me that felt real.

## ARCHETYPES IN FILMS AND TELEVISION

Television programs, magazines and films have a lot to teach us about archetypes; in today's world the media are our link to the collective unconscious, and how people relate to them reveals much about themselves and their longings. If one of my clients mentions a particular television program, I will ask what aspect of it they identify with. As they describe their attraction to or interest in a particular character, their answers often give me a sense of their archetypal processes.

With such strong visual stimulation from television, films and advertisements, today's archetypes appear in the form of image setters as well as heroes. The archetypes presented in the media contain the very best and worst of human endeavor, reflecting the qualities valued in our time. It is interesting that many of our current popular films are stories of scams and cons; they seem to reflect, at some unconscious level, the permissiveness and greed of our society with their implicit message that it is acceptable to be dishonest as long as you don't get caught.

Fortunately, there are also many positive archetypes in today's popular media. Present-day archetypes, though wearing modern dress, face moral and ethical dilemmas which are universal themes, transcending time and fashion. As we watch the movie or read the story, whether it is Rambo who takes on the enemy or Sir Gawain from the Arthurian legend, we learn about opposition, courage and steadfastness. The fascination so many people find in soap operas lies in their on-going stories of struggles for power and triumphs over adversity, while their characters often portray recognizable archetypes including Victims and Warriors, Mothers and Empresses. How their heroes and heroines cope with their personal problems and form or dissolve relationships affects audiences deeply, and can, indeed, be helpful by the examples they offer.

Recently, a middle-aged friend of mine suffered a marriage breakdown. During her initial period of grief she saw on television a wonderfully sensitive story about a middle-aged woman whose husband fell in love with a younger woman. The story of how she managed to cope and live through the situation was touching and encouraging, as it showed her confronting her grief and anger, and eventually regaining her self-esteem. It not only presented the universal archetype of an age-old dilemma faced by many women, it also offered them courage and support by presenting a kind of emotional blueprint as to how to handle one's grief and bewilderment and rebuild one's life.

This, too, was an archetypal situation, in which the heroine moved from the archetype of Victim to that of Warrior through facing her challenges. It enabled my friend to see that there could be a positive outcome: that she could survive this ordeal and come through intact, with her life ahead of her. This was a truly positive example of learning from an archetypal story.

# TWO-DIMENSIONALITY AND INDIVIDUALITY

Archetypes can reflect the deeper aspects of our emotional nature. If we allow them to show us our front, or lighter, side they will also show us our back, or darker, sides. They are a template for what is good and healthy in us, as well as what is dark and neurotic in our personalities. They are, basically, a two-dimensional portrait of our individual attitudes.

We can see this in the myths of good and evil we come to know as children, in which the Hero and the Villain are portrayed in strictly black and white terms. We seldom see archetypes in the more variable shades of human nature. As with all models, archetypes are simply a map and are not the territory. They offer, in a pure form, an approach to the life issues we all face, but they lack the multi-dimensional characters of real people, and the limitless choices and creative possibilities available to us.

Jung has been quoted as saying, "Never identify with your archetype." I think he meant that to do so would detract from our humanness and individuality. When we become too strongly identified with the role we are playing, we lose the three-dimensionality of our individual self, and with it our freedom of choice. When a man tries to act too much like Rambo at the expense of his feelings, or a woman emulates a glamorous film star at the cost of her natural beauty, he or she loses what is quintessential in themselves.

It is in the nature of archetypes to be bigger than life, but they are not three-dimensional, they are not human; they are the purest essence of a characterization. An archetype will never disappoint you: his or her choices and reactions are always predictable. Rambo is not going to let down millions of fans by suddenly realizing that the enemy is just an outward projection of his inner emotional state so that he can develop his higher consciousness. He is not going to stop fighting and start loving his fellow man. Rambo needs his opposition in order to keep alive the myth of the Invincible Warrior.

Individuals, by contrast, are unique. We are all a composite of the light and the dark, the good and the bad. It is important to avoid personal identification with a set of archetypes, and accept your own individuality. Archetypes are here to serve your growth and consciousness through helping you to identify any patterns which may block your true nature. They are not and never could be who you are, because they do not encompass the totality of your personality.

# ARCHETYPES AS RITES OF PASSAGE

All human cultures have celebrated the conscious evolution of the soul. We have, in fact, created archetypes to reflect the different stages of our emotional development. They symbolize rites of passage towards wholeness and integration. In the esoteric schools of philosophy this process of achieving oneness is called initiation. It occurs when we transcend our current archetypes and move on towards higher levels of spiritual awareness.

We have with us the possibility of realizing all the archetypes, whether they are dominant or passive in our personalities. As we develop and progress along our path in life we can draw on the energy of new, higher archetypes which emerge from the shadow of our personality to serve and assist us in our spiritual awakening.

For example, when we begin actively to create what we want in our lives—such as love, health and happiness—our new-found sense of entitlement takes us out of the Victim or Martyr archetype into a more positive state, such as that of the Empress or the Warrior. Each process of transcending an archetype completes a cycle of initiation.

We cannot grow to our fullest potential without passing through every stage of development, each of which has its own archetype. We look to these universal archetypes to see what is normal at any particular stage: for example the archetype of the happy, carefree child is followed by the rebellious adolescent, then the responsible adult, and finally the wise and mature elder. If, for some reason, we diverge from the archetypal role appropriate to our stage of development, we may need help to regain our balance.

For example, many of us contain within us the Silent Child: that part of our psyche which has been damaged or hurt by the past, and cannot respond to new or positive situations because it has become stuck in the patterns of fear or intimidation. But when we use the archetypes as a guide to the inner process of discovering who we are, they help us to become our own Healer and Guru. Through acknowledging and nourishing our ability to care for and understand ourselves, we can embody the Mother archetype which gives us the possibility of healing this Silent Child. Through releasing the pain of this wound, whatever has been arrested and thwarted is allowed to heal and grow. Then the Child can flourish, and continue to mature in a creative and spiritual way.

## THE NEED TO MOVE ON

For us to complete our journey, the positive aspects of the archetypes also need to be transcended. Most of us get stuck at certain stages of life. For example, in order to succeed, a young man starting out in business will need courage, willpower and determination, and possibly also cunning and aggression. In other words, he will cultivate the qualities of the Warrior archetype, and as his career progresses he will incorporate them into his personality.

He may spend a good part of his life at this level of development. However, his archetype can and should change as he matures, through finding love, creativity, self-control and spirituality. This will happen easily if he is open to his growth process. If, however, he is resistant to change and avoids facing emotional challenges, he may remain arrested at a lower level. He may marry because that is expected of him, but will remain focused on his personal power.

If he fails to choose love, he is likely to have experiences in his life that will push him towards that which he resists. These may take the form of an illness, or perhaps an external event like a car accident or a major setback in business. Whatever the trigger, it will make him aware of his need for closer relationships with others. Once he chooses to grow emotionally, he will transcend his Warrior archetype and draw on the qualities of a new archetype, the Lover, exchanging his focus on power in order to become more loving. He can then go on to seek higher levels of refinement, spirituality and empowerment when he incorporates love into his life.

Similarly, many women are cast in the role of the Mother for a long period of their lives. This is a positive archetype, but there comes a stage when a woman needs to transcend that role. She may come to realize that in giving too much to others she is enacting the Servant, or perhaps the Martyr who blames others for her dissatisfaction. She can choose to embody the Empress by valuing her own femininity, sexuality and pleasure in life. She can also move into the Warrior archetype by learning how to stand up for herself and negotiate in the world—perhaps by getting a job, attending an assertiveness course or studying for a degree.

Transcending these positive archetypes does not mean that we leave them behind. When we have moved beyond the Mother or the Warrior, their qualities are still there for us to draw on when needed. But they are now differentiated; that is, we are conscious of them instead of letting them run our lives. And as we continue to progress, the archetypes will also change in quality; our inner Mother will develop and eventually become the Wise Woman.

It is important not to skip stages on this journey. There are many people seeking spiritual growth who may have wonderful experiences through meditation and other spiritual practices. But we cannot leap from the Victim to the Guru and expect to remain at that high level if we have bypassed other aspects of ourselves. Until we have worked our way through all archetypal stages of development, life will bring up situations that will force us to pay attention to any parts of ourselves which need healing and transformation.

Sometimes the same archetype will re-emerge repeatedly. There are many situations in which I find myself feeling helpless, alone and unable to cope, and my Victim archetype repeatedly emerges. Over time, however, I have become able to identify it as it appears, and realize that it comes up whenever I deny my own sense of power. Once I remind myself that I am not a Victim, I am able to stand up for myself and handle whatever is needed with humour and dignity.

With time and repetition I realize I can transform this archetype and create a more conscious and empowered one for myself. As I evolve emotionally and spiritually, new archetypes have emerged in my conscious mind. This new awareness is reflected in my daily activities and particularly in my relationships. This happens increasingly as I take more and more responsibility for my life, and allow myself to experience what I am feeling.

# 2

# ARCHETYPES AND
# THE CHAKRAS

At first, connecting archetypes with human relationships and emotional development was only an intellectual concept for me. But as I went on to work in homoeopathy and bioenergetic therapy, both forms of healing which help release deep emotional blockages, I experienced for myself the strong connection between the archetypal roles and the attitudes people play out in their lives, and the energetic and emotional states they experience. I saw that people who were manifesting clearer and stronger archetypes also had stronger and higher states of energy.

For example, from my own experiences and my work with other people it became clear that the Victim has minimal energy. The Warrior, by contrast—the workaholic businessman or woman, for instance—may have ruthless energy in his or her career, but little left for family and intimate relationships. On the other hand, when I met a Guru, a spiritual teacher, in India, I was deeply impressed by the abundance of energy which poured from him and the intimate connections with one another that everyone experienced in his presence. There was no sense of exclusiveness or separateness at this level of consciousness, only a wondrous sense of belonging and a deep connection with one's self and others. The energy level was so high, yet peaceful and centered, it was distinct from anything I had previously experienced.

The Guru demonstrated a major shift in awareness from the Warrior archetype, and a level of development I definitely wanted to know more about. It struck me that there must be a direct connection between people's energy and the archetype they were living out.

# HOW ATTITUDES CAN HURT OR HEAL US

The relationship of the archetypes to our emotional and physical well-being is closely linked to our attitudes about ourselves and life. Simply stated, energy follows thought. When we feel good about ourselves and accept who we are with love and a gracious spirit, we create the space for good things to happen in our lives. When we fail to love ourselves we leave an opening for negative experiences to come our way.

What you think about not only affects how you feel about yourself: it creates experiences in your life which correspond to those feelings. When you believe something to be true, your experiences will fall into line with your belief. In other words, your attitudes and opinions attract things to you like a magnet.

People and situations offer us opportunities to experience what we believe about ourselves. Every situation is a challenge and a gift from our Higher Self, the positive template of our fullest potential, to look at what is good and pure within us. We have the ability to change our ideas about our thoughts and feelings whenever we honor ourselves, and realize that we are truly worthy of love, tenderness and respect.

One way to affirm ourselves is by examining our attitudes and, if necessary, changing those which are negative. When we change our feelings about ourselves to become more positive and affirmative, our energy changes: we lighten up and look and feel good. Other people pick up on our vibration and affirm our good feelings about ourselves.

Frankly speaking, the choice is ours and ours alone, as to what we want life to be and what we want to do with our experiences. We can learn and grow from every experience in our life or we can stay locked in blame and rejection. But whatever you think or feel about yourself and others is reflected in your energy.

This is the working principle by which archetypes and their related energy centers, known as chakras, function in the human energy system. Whenever we have problems with a particular issue, such as lack of self-love, this will be reflected in lowered energy in the relevant chakra, and a need to work with the related archetype.

# WORKING WITH THE CHAKRAS

There are seven main chakras in the human energy system, aligned up the spine from the base to the crown of the head. They are non-anatomical vortices of energy which exist just outside and within the physical body at what is called the etheric level of the aura; this lies outside of and interpenetrates our physical body.

Their purpose is to filter energy throughout our system so that we have enough vitality to live our lives. Each of the seven chakras relates to a particular ductless gland and specific organ in its area, supplementing them with life energy channeled from the cosmos and the earth. If one or more is blocked, life energy will not flow freely through our system, and we can develop physical problems in that area.

Each relates not only to the health energy of the physical body but also to specific emotional issues. Each has encoded within it the pattern of our attitudes which are blocking the life force or allowing it to flow freely. It is our thoughts and attitudes, more than anything else, which block or release the flow of energy through the chakras.

The degree of positive or negative energy within each chakra corresponds to the archetype we are presently living out in our lives. Both archetypes and chakras reflect a direct link between how well we love ourselves, and our levels of vitality, responsibility and empowerment. They reveal the qualities in ourselves which shine in the Light of Self, and those that are in need of greater awareness and development.

Each chakra holds within it a negative or dysfunctional archetype as well as a positive, functional one. Its level of vitality, well-being and awareness is associated with the archetype it embraces. They begin with the Victim, which has little vitality and empowerment and is associated with a dysfunctional root chakra; at the top end of this scale is the Guru, which is light, free, full of vitality and totally empowered and is connected with the Crown chakra.

Thus, working with the chakras helps us to understand where our energy is blocked, while working with the archetypes shows us which attitudes or emotional issues we need to examine in order to move on to the next, higher stage.

# THE SEVEN MAIN CHAKRAS, AND THEIR RELATED EMOTIONS AND ARCHETYPES

**1—The Root Chakra** is located at the base of the spine in the area of the tailbone. This chakra filters energy up from the earth and connects our higher energies to the basic reality of life. The emotional issues relating to this chakra revolve around the essentials we need for survival and our sense of security in the world. This includes the shelter of a home to protect us, financial security and adequate food to nourish ourselves. We also need good emotional ties with our family, friends, community and country. This chakra becomes damaged when we lose our connection to Mother Earth; in other words, when we become disconnected from the most basic human levels of existence.

Related to the root chakra are the dysfunctional archetype of the **Victim**, and the functional archetype of the **Mother**.

**2—The Sacral Chakra** is located in the lower abdomen about 2 inches below the navel and 2 inches in. In Eastern philosophy this center is known as the Hara, and it plays an essential part in the Asian martial arts as the central focus for movement and co-ordination.

At an emotional level, it governs our sense of abundance, well-being, pleasure and sexuality. It is a center which has been highly exploited in our society, and no one in our Western culture has perfect function in this chakra. A basic attitude of well-being and having enough are associated with a healthy sacral chakra.

The dysfunctional archetype connected with this chakra is the **Martyr**; the functional archetype is the **Empress/Emperor**.

**3—The Solar Plexus Chakra** is located in the upper abdomen in the region of the stomach. It energizes the organs of digestion and helps us to sensitize ourselves to our environment. The emotional issues of the Solar Plexus are focused on self-worth, self-esteem, self-confidence and personal power. It is therefore connected with our attitudes towards empowerment and decision-making. When we value ourselves, we have a well-functioning Solar Plexus. At present, many people are focusing on releasing the dysfunctional power issues which affect this chakra.

The **Servant** is the dysfunctional archetype of the Solar Plexus, and the **Warrior** the functional one.

**4—The Heart Chakra** is located in the center of chest above the region of the physical heart. It relates, of course, to love and joy. The healthy functioning of this chakra allows us to form loving bonds with people in the world around us and to reach out to others. People with open hearts are a blessing in any family or community; they teach us about love and kindness, and how to forgive ourselves and others for any lack of love or caring.

The dysfunctional archetype of the Heart chakra is the **Actor/Actress**, and the functional archetype is the **Lover**.

**5—The Throat Chakra** is located inside the throat, where it acts as the bridge between our minds and our hearts. It is the center of communication, creativity, self-expression, willpower and truth; its purpose is to allow clear and effective communication, and to enhance our creative spirit. When we are able to express our feelings clearly and honestly our throat center is open, and we feel alive and expressive. If, for any reason, we are blocked in expressing ourselves, this center becomes congested. This can lead to health problems focused in the throat, mouth and sinus areas.

The dysfunctional archetype of this center is the **Silent Child**, and the functional one is the **Communicator**.

**6—The Brow Chakra** is located in the forehead between the eyebrows. It governs our ability to think and discern, use our intuition and imagination, and gather wisdom from our life experiences. It is also known as the control center, because it is thoughts and attitudes which enable us to change our perceptions and ideas about how life is, or how we think it should be. When we reflect positively on life, we begin to build a strong spiritual life.

The dysfunctional archetype of the Brow chakra is the **Intellectual**, and the functional archetype is the **Wise Person**.

**7—The Crown Chakra** is located at the very crown of the head, and links us with beauty, refinement and our spiritual nature. It channels energy from the heavens into the physical body, starting the process of the downward flow of energy which grounds the spirit in the body. This chakra grows and develops as we mature, and opens us to the Source within.

The dysfunctional archetype of the Crown is the **Egotist**, and the functional archetype is the **Guru**.

# HOW CHAKRAS AFFECT OUR HEALTH AND HAPPINESS

The chakras are conductors of energy; healthy chakras allow energy to flow freely through our physical and emotional bodies and our energetic system. The flow of life energy may be stopped, however, by negativity, often by the negative thought "and the media.

It is said in Chinese medicine that we inherit our life force from both our parents. Sometimes a life vision or attitude is deeply rooted in the family history, and in order to grow and live creatively, we may be forced to bring into our own consciousness the unexpressed anger, fear or grief which stopped our parents from living their lives to the fullest.

As we develop our consciousness, what may have been seen as an acceptable attitude in the family becomes no longer viable. When we are emotionally blocked by these old attitudes, the flow of energy in the chakras slows down and inhibits our physical vitality. If these blocks are not released through some form of physical or emotional expression, they can impede the life flow so severely that we become ill or unbalanced.

As we have seen, the archetypes, which are very closely linked to the chakras, are a collection of attitudes and ideas that also have a direct relationship with our levels of health and well-being. Our state of happiness and health is therefore dependent upon our thinking, by how positive we are, and by our ability and willingness to discharge blocked energy.

In Chapter 1 we looked at the example of a young man starting off in business. In terms of the chakras, in order to cultivate the qualities of the Warrior archetype, his vital energy will be focused in his Solar Plexus, the center of personal power. If he has problems in developing his sense of power, integrity and self-worth, he may develop health problems in this area, perhaps in the liver, stomach or small intestine. At a later stage, the businessman who resists developing his capacity for loving, focused in the heart center may find himself suffering from problems in the area of the Heart chakra.

There is clear evidence that energy shifts when we change our attitudes. The more accepting and loving we are of ourselves and our lives, the quicker our energy opens up and starts to flow. When positive patterns replace outworn negative ones in our minds, then our energy can shift to a lighter, freer level, expressed in a sense of freedom, joy and ease. When we begin to accept ourselves we feel better about everything, and are happier and healthier.

One way we can tell that blocked energy is impeding our happiness is when we are in a situation which offers all the potential for fun and happiness, and yet find that we are fearful, blocked or critical. We are then experiencing our own limitations and negative responses. By looking at our emotional response we can identify which chakras are blocked and which archetype we are playing out. We then have the option of starting the healing process. Rather than creating further damage by getting into the rut of punishing and judging ourselves, we can focus love, warmth, gentleness and understanding on those wounded parts of ourselves.

## CHOOSING LOVE AND POSITIVE ATTITUDES

It is up to us to choose at which level of awareness we wish to see ourselves. There is certainly more joy and serenity when we live our lives from the highest intention to be all that we can be, and to love others as we would wish to be loved. But to reach this state, we all have old patterns which block our well-being and need to be changed. Personal growth and spiritual development is about moving through those impediments.

For those who choose not to look at themselves, and weed out their negative projections and blame, it is a shame both for themselves and for those close to them. There is truly nothing more disheartening and frustrating than watching friends and loved ones act out the same old, tired games over and over again. By the same token, people who are working on themselves, whatever level of awareness they are at, are uplifting and joyful to be around because they are taking responsibility for who they are, and making a real effort for their lives to work and to find happiness for themselves.

Life, if we choose, always gives us the opportunity to trust in our highest good and greatest joy. Every situation we are in, whether it involves a personal or a working relationship, asks us to trust in ourselves and let go of our negativity. This can get momentarily uncomfortable or even painful, but ultimately it serves us to feel our feelings and let go of the impediments to our joy and aliveness.

When we love ourselves, and forgive and bless others, we are open to enchantment, joy and serenity in our lives; everything flows better. The degree to which we value ourselves and are able to express our feelings reflects a more developed archetype and a higher level of well-being and happiness. We learn how to discern what is right and good for us.

If you want to grow from your experiences, watch how you feel, and pay attention to your actions, behavior and dreams: these are the best indicators of your attitudes and innermost feelings. They are the reflectors of your basic beliefs about yourself and life. They help you to see where and how you are stuck. If you are willing to do some work on yourself, you can release inappropriate attitudes so that you can live your life well and from the depths of your true self.

The rest of this book is devoted to taking you through each chakra, and its related negative and positive archetypes. By healing our energetic state we transform our archetypes, and become more in tune with the universal forces which move through us, enriching our lives and letting us be the creative spirits we truly are.

## HOW TO USE THIS BOOK

The next seven chapters take you on a journey through the chakras and their related archetypes, both negative and positive. I suggest that you work through all of them in order, using them as stepping stones to your growth and spiritual development. As you ascend the ladder of awareness and take more personal responsibility for yourself, you will find that you have much more energy and vitality, as well as a deeper sense of self-empowerment.

Each chapter describes a particular chakra, and the negative and positive archetypes associated with it, together with two case studies, based on people I have worked with, illustrating the types of situation people face as they live out their archetypes.

I then go on to give exercises that will help you to release old archetypal patterns. Also included is a meditation, intended to encourage peace and acceptance, which will help to release any fears that may arise from seeing aspects of yourself with which you are not at ease.

This is followed by a series of affirmations to focus your mind and feelings into a positive mode. Affirmations are useful for focusing your intention about what you want in your life. They help you to release any negative patterns you may have associated with the archetype.

By working through the chakras in this way, you have the opportunity to heal any negative archetypes, which represent the areas in which you may be stuck in

This chapter looks at the distinction between the two Root chakra archetypes, the Victim and the Mother, and offers constructive exercises for grounding your spirit in your body so that it is easier to maintain a healthy foundation for developing yourself and refining higher energy states, to stay rooted in reality and maintain your connection to your deep inner core. Without grounding, your grasp of the higher energies will be tenuous and it will not be possible to sustain them without plummeting back towards earth and *reality*. From a healthy base within, you can connect with your feelings, experience your body and relate to others.

## What Is Grounding?

One of the principles of grounding is "to get out of our heads and into our bodies." According to Alexander Lowen, the founder of Bioenergetic Therapy, and his mentor, Wilhelm Reich, it is through the life of the body that we are able to experience pleasure and pain, and connect with our feelings. Only by maintaining a direct and conscious link with our physical body can we discharge the accumulated emotional energy of our daily lives. Without grounding our energy in some form of expression, our emotions become stagnant and stuck, so that we stay fixed and inflexible, unable to meet new challenges with vigor and vitality. Without this connection with our body we become "lost in space", unable to define our reality and who we are.

People who live in the realm of fantasy and conjecture (whom we might describe as *spaced out*), are not grounded. They are disconnected from their feelings and are unable to deal with either their anger or their joy. They have a poor grasp on life, and can fail to care for themselves properly. Grounding means that all the basic life support systems are properly maintained, and there is shelter, food, money and clothing for keeping our physical world intact.

When we lose our grounding or contact with reality we become victims. The way this manifests is that it becomes impossible for us to manage our lives and such things as work, shelter and other basic needs. Everything becomes a struggle.

The way through this archetypal state is to reconnect with our inner being, that part of ourselves which is eternal and permanent, and bring back awareness into our body. This connection with the inner core grounds the spirit, and sensing our body puts us in touch with our feelings. From this place we are able to make realistic decisions based on our highest good and greatest joy. We are then able to let go of our attachments to life being a certain way and more able to go with the flow to facilitate the changes we need to make. When we are flexible and fluid we stop trying to control how our lives should unfold.

One of the ways we can do this is by consciously breathing and moving so that we do not become stuck in either a rigid stance or a fixed attitude. This helps us release terror and fear, shame and guilt or other emotions which stand in the way of our being truly grounded.

## *Dysfunctional Archetype: The Victim*

### Recognizing The Victim

The lowest level of energy and awareness is the Victim archetype. The Victim experiences itself at the mercy of outside forces which work against it. It seldom has awareness or a sense of responsibility for its circumstances. The Victim feels that "something happened to me".

Victims suffer because, it appears to them, all choice has been taken from them and their fate is completely outside of their control. The Victim archetype is in a helpless state, totally reliant on the external world represented by a partner, companion, family, group of people or an organization, and disconnected from their inner core of feelings. The Victim's mind is stuck in a frozen state of fear, terror or desperation, with no sense of empowerment.

These are powerful emotions and they can cripple anyone who identifies with them. They can be so overwhelming as to break the connection between our ground of being and our spirit. Being a Victim is paralyzing in its effect on the psyche and the body.

In order to survive, both emotionally and physically, it is essential to ground these feelings and to reconnect with the basic simplicity and goodness of life. Being in the moment and trusting in life's processes helps to avoid falling into the Victim archetype. Using drugs, alcohol or suppressive medication only disconnects us even more from the core of our feelings and instincts. In order to survive we need our wits about us, to feel ourselves rooted in the body, and to trust in our highest good unfolding, whatever that may be.

Often circumstances combine to put Victims outside of the mainstream of either hope or help. Events such as divorce, illness, death, prison and bankruptcy can easily uproot and unground people and make them feel like a Victim.

If the life force is strong we will engage with life's challenges and meet them head on, knowing we will survive and master our circumstances. If our life force, however, is not strong or is weakened, than we can easily fall pray to victimhood. The tragedy of this is the loss of so much joy and goodness to humanity. When people are given the chance to live and thrive their creative resources flourish. This is evidenced by national or cultural groups who have been uprooted and forced to start again. This takes tenacity, willpower and courage, and often means making sacrifices and mistakes along the way.

Ethnic groups such as Jews, Vietnamese, Africans, Chileans and Bosnians have been uprooted from their native lands and forced to start their lives over in new places. Many of these peoples have both a strong life force and a strong spiritual will to sustain them through upheaval and tragedy. They have learned to reconnect their energy and creativity back in to the life force in enterprising and productive ways, and many have avoided becoming Victims. What they have made of their lives is, in part, dependent on their personal and spiritual attitudes, and their feelings of entitlement.

If they feel they have the right to survive and flourish they will manage to overcome all odds and succeed. If they are in doubt about their rights what they ask of life will be minimal and it will always be a struggle to regain their lost roots and sense of self worth. When such negative attitudes remain suppressed, they get passed on to their children and grandchildren to be made conscious. It is often the second or third generation of immigrants who have to sort out the emotional realities of past generations' traumas.

### Emotional Victims

Victims exist at many levels. Emotional Victims are people who have a difficult time re-establishing their lives after tragedy, separation or loss. Because of their vulnerability, they are susceptible to illness and plagued with problems which anyone in normal circumstances would find easy to handle, but which the Victim finds daunting and nearly impossible.

Many people may not be aware that they carry traces of the Victim mentality within their personality. These roots can emerge in times of stress or crisis. If they were to stop and experience the feelings they have about life they might be surprised at the depths of the anger, fear, resentment and frustration they carry inside them.

The attitude which makes a Victim is that someone else is responsible, or something has been done to them. Their power has been snatched away and their choices negated. They are at the mercy of what others say and do to them. Of course, it is these feelings of blame, shame and guilt which create broken spirits and severe emotional stress.

Often emotional Victims find themselves beset by events which appear to be beyond their control. Sometimes it appears as though they were asking the universe to collude with their lack of self esteem and to prove that they have little or no personal empowerment by creating trying circumstances for them to cope with.

Yet, it is these very circumstances which challenge the Victim archetype to become empowered and to help them say that they have had enough of this way of being treated. This transforms them into spiritual warriors capable of dealing with life. It helps them to stand up for themselves and to negotiate life on their terms.

It is also the willingness to reframe life's circumstances into opportunity, rather than loss, which helps people rise above victimhood. Nearly everyone is given the opportunity to face such challenges with their health, finances or relationships at some point in their lives, for how else do we grow emotionally and mature into whole and integrated people? It is through tackling these difficult circumstances that we develop into wise and compassionate beings.

### Beginning to change the Victim mentality

Mobility is the key to understanding the Victim mentality and the Root chakra governs our capacity to mobilize our body. Victims move either too slowly, with great trepidation and fear, or they move too quickly and compulsively, not putting their feet down where they belong. The message the body gives us is to experience and release our feelings so that we can be free and aware of the ground under our feet.

The Victim also needs to be helped to regain a sense of choice. The other, and perhaps more important, thing is to change the idea that the Victim is at the mercy of other people or a situation. By reframing the Victim's thoughts into positive statements about their lives, they can turn their energy around and begin to release it back into the life force, thus being empowered to freely choose what is best for them. This, more than anything, helps the Victim archetype transform itself.

# MOVING ON FROM THE VICTIM ARCHETYPE

## Taking Responsibility For Yourself

You can change your archetype when you take responsibility for your attitudes and ideas. From here, anyone with a Victim mentality can begin to feel they have a chance. When we acknowledge the truth about our lives we automatically own our power.

We all have choices in our lives. The *where, when* and *how* of life are often the result of how we feel about ourselves, and how worthy we feel to attract the love and good fortune we need. When life does not give us what we feel we deserve we can become Victims or we can attempt to understand what these obstacles have to tell us about our life's journey. It is from taking responsibility for where we are and how we feel that we regain our sense of choice and can move forward in life.

We all have the opportunity to learn and grow through difficult or trying circumstances. It can, however, take time to release the grief, sadness and anger associated with change. It is always worth looking back at any situation and asking what we learned about ourselves and life from it. This is a positive way of freeing ourselves from victimhood.

The first thing to do in any situation where you feel like a Victim is to be honest about your feelings. This simple-sounding, yet difficult task, frees you from delusion and begins your process towards empowerment. When you can tell the truth about how you are feeling you begin to liberate yourself from the burden of negativity in your life. You may be caught in a difficult situation where you are experiencing loss, pain or separation. This is the moment when you need to tell yourself the truth about what you feel. It is from here you allow sadness, anger, anxiety or joy to be expressed.

## Exercise

1 Recall an experience in your life where you felt like a Victim. This would be a time when something happened to you which was out of your control and left you feeling hurt or unsure of yourself.

2 What are your feelings about this situation now? Are you angry, enraged, sad, grieving? Are you willing to tell yourself more about how you feel regarding this situation? Be willing to take the lid off your feelings and experience them as they are.

3 Look at other people and situations in your life that have made you feel as though you were a Victim. In your mind's eye withdraw the energy you have invested in them and take your power back into yourself. The way you do that is to say: "What I feel about … is … and I freely chose to release myself from these negative feelings."

4 As you take responsibility for the people and situations in your life think about what your projections were. You can do this by identifying the themes running through your story and see that what looks like blame may be your projection into someone or a situation so that you could experience an underlying attitude you had about yourself.

   For instance, you may say that someone didn't love you enough or respect you enough. To own your projection it becomes necessary to say that there was a part of you that didn't love yourself enough or respect yourself enough. By projecting our attitudes onto others we make them responsible for fulfilling our expectations. By looking at our projections, we can heal that part of ourselves which is unloved and neglected. Learning to love yourself through difficult situations empowers you and gives you the freedom to be yourself.

   Are you willing to move on to do a meditation to help you release more of your feelings? (This is an important question. If you are not willing to release your feelings please take responsibility for this. Either way it will empower you to know you have a choice.)

## The Myth Of The Victim Archetype

The *myth* sections in each chapter will help you to identify some of the themes running through the various archetypes and in turn enable you to identify some of your own attitudes which may be attached to these archetypes.

If you look at your attitudes surrounding the people and situations which have contributed to your experience of victimhood you may begin to see patterns that make you aware of how this happened in your life. Is there a connection between your attitudes to sacrifice and suffering and your present experience? Such attitudes may come from myths you have held about your family, your parents, early education or religion and are worth examining because they form the matrix of emotional energy upon which all your relationships are based. We can fall into the Victim archetype when we feel that others owe us something or we feel we owe others more than they deserve.

The way to change attitudes like these is simple. You begin by asking yourself what are your beliefs about the following. Are you entitled to:

Happiness?

Respect?

Health? (includes your feelings about beauty, fitness and aging.)

Love?

Money?

Friendship?

Success?

Do you feel supported in having what you want in life?

If you feel any negativity about these things, examine your attitudes carefully and reframe those which do not support your desires. These negative attitudes stand in the way of you having what you want and deserve. To empower yourself in life, it is important that you believe you are entitled to all the good life can offer and that you can fully enjoy it.

# MEDITATION

Sit or lie in a comfortable position where you can relax and be at ease. Burn incense and light a candle if you like, to cleanse the energy around you and help you relax your mind. Close your eyes and take a deep breath. Release any tension from your neck and shoulders as you release your breath by breathing in through your nose and out from your mouth, releasing your jaw as you breathe out. Go through your body and release tension wherever you find it. It may be lodged at the back of your neck, behind your eyes or in your throat. It may be in your back, hips or ankles. Take your time to breathe deeply and let go of your tension.

As you continue to breathe deeply remember a situation or a person who made you feel like a Victim. Take one incident at a time. Do not overwhelm yourself or become dismayed, believing bad things are always happening to you.

As you see this person or situation in your mind's eye ask yourself what you are feeling. Allow your feelings to come to the surface. You may experience hatred, anger, fear or grief, or you could actually find the situation or person humorous now and realize that you have released your negative feelings already.

Consciously deepen your breathing as you allow your feelings to come into consciousness. Now say to yourself:

*I acknowledge my feelings about … and I release them.*
*I am free of negative thoughts about this person or situation. I am free. I am now in charge of my life. I will consciously be sure to never give away my power again. I know that I have grown and developed wisdom from having had this experience in my life. I look forward to facing my life free from negative emotions about this situation. I now live in peace, joy and serenity, and I hope the person who caused these emotions is as well.*

Visualize the negative feelings passing out of your body and being released into the ether like smoke. Trust this energy will be recycled and that this learning has all been for your good.

Now visualize that person or situation. Say to whomever you see: "I forgive you, I bless you and I set you free." Repeat this as many times as you need to in order to feel the impact of these words.

*I forgive you, I bless you and I set you free.*

Imagine that the place in you where you stored the hurt is now an empty space waiting to be filled with light and beautiful colors. The pain may have been lodged in your heart or in your shoulder blades, your hips or your solar plexus. Release it with your breath. See the colors filling this empty space, and bringing ease and comfort into that part of you which has been constricted and tight.

Colors carry energy and signify emotional qualities. Violet is for the spirit, blue is the universal healing color, turquoise is the color of creativity, green is for peace, pink is for mother love, yellow is for intelligence, orange is for vitality and red is for passion. Flood the area of your pain with these colors. You may wish to add gold or silver to the richness these colors bring you. Acknowledge to yourself that even though you did not like or approve of what happened to you, you are stronger and wiser for having been through this experience in your life. Without this experience you would not have developed into the person you are. When you allow yourself to do this, you begin healing the wounds which linked you to the Victim archetype. Use this meditation any time you feel you are a Victim.


## Vitality

If you have been experiencing yourself as a Victim, you may have also found you were either physically immobilized or hyperactive for some time. When you feel that you are a Victim you are seldom at ease and free of tension in your body—you are not grounded. It helps to start moving easily and gently to get your energy flowing again and re-establish your grounding. It is important, as well, to choose to do something which will give you pleasure and not impose punishment or strain. You have probably given yourself enough of that already.

You may want to do something as simple as going for a walk down the street or a major expedition into the wilderness. Think about what you enjoy doing and then go for it. Give yourself a goal that is attainable so that you can give yourself the pleasure of achieving something you truly want. Here are some suggestions.

Go for a walk

Dance

Work-out

Swim

Play tennis or squash

Jog

Do yoga or aerobics

Have a massage or some form of body therapy which is gentle and non-intrusive

Go camping

Do some gardening

Practice Tai Chi

Take a holiday to a place you have always wished to visit

Whatever you do, be good to yourself and persevere with your activity. It is important if you have felt like a Victim to re-establish the flow of energy. Don't push yourself, just be encouraged to get out and move.

Some of the activities I have suggested may seem strenuous to you. The more aggression and anger you have about your situation as a Victim the better it is to let the energy pass out of your system. Once you have started to take responsibility for yourself you will feel better. However, if you have been moving too fast and have not had an opportunity to experience your feelings you may feel tired and want to slow down. Honor your body and give your emotions the space they deserve.

## Empowerment

Affirmations can help you reframe your attitudes about yourself and any situation in which you have felt victimized. As you integrate their positive message into your consciousness they will help you feel empowered. This means that you can start to take charge of your life. You begin to take back some or all of the power you invested in this situation.

You can write down the affirmations several times a day, tell them to yourself while you are driving to and from work, or say them to yourself in front of a mirror. Let the energy of their positive force work to heal you.

*I am a child of the universe and I am always loved and protected.*

*I affirm that I am strong and able to handle any situation.*

*I am thankful for this opportunity to express myself and grow. Right now I feel good about myself.*

*The universe supports my growth and development. This situation has taught me to be free and happy with myself.*

*I honor myself at all times. I am now doing the very best for myself that I possibly can.*

*I release all negative feelings that hold me back from being happy and free.*

*I forgive and release the past and live in the here and now.*

*I choose the present and fill it with fun, joy and light.*

*I bless all those who have helped me realize my worth along the path of light.*

*The universe is a safe and benign place for me to be. I am always protected and guided. I know that I belong.*

*I trust in the good. I allow it to enter my life.*

*I take responsibility for who I am and how my life is.*

*I am safe. I honor my need for kindness, love and respect.*

*I honor my need for gentleness, care and consideration.*

*I am not a Victim. I am on the path of light which is rich in personal experience.*

*I love and honor who I am. I am thankful for my life.*

## Case Histories

### Inelia

Inelia was a middle-aged woman from a South American country taken over by a military dictatorship when she was a young mother. She and her husband were rounded up by military police and separated, and she was put into the squalor of an over-filled prison with minimal facilities. She languished in prison for several months. She was badly tortured and left for weeks in solitary confinement. She would sing for several hours every day to keep her sanity.

One day without any reason she was released. She eventually found her children but did not see her husband for many years. She gathered her courage and, with help, came to Europe. She found employment as a teacher and educated her children. At the age of 52 she suddenly decided to embark on a course of training as a homeopath which would allow her to fulfill her inquisitive mind and probing nature. She said that she felt privileged to be able to choose what she wanted to do at this point in her life. She was happy her life had turned out so well and that her children had the opportunity to develop into the people she had hoped they could become.

Anyone who met Inelia noticed her winning smile and happy demeanor. She was never willing to be a Victim even through the most horrible of times and her faith in life remained unshakable. She told a story that while she was alone in a prison cell she saw an angel appear before her. She said it was luminescent and exquisite. It told her that she would be released and have her life before her again. She has always felt a profound sense of gratitude for the opportunity to rebuild her life.

Sadly, Inelia died recently. She was surrounded by a group of women friends. For these women knowing her was a source of inspiration. She was a shining example of the ability of the human spirit to transcend difficulties.

## Paul

Paul, now in his early fifties, was an abused child from a dysfunctional home. He was battered and neglected by his parents, who acted out their own unhappiness and frustration on him. He realized there was a larger world than the narrow and bleak one his family inhabited, and he was determined to leave as soon as he could. When he was 14 he ran away from home and hitched rides around Europe, living on practically no money.

When he had saved some money he left for India. He stayed in an ashram for eight years, studying and growing. He wanted to do something to help others and came back to the West to train in osteopathy. He eventually settled in a small town where he knew a few people and started his practice.

He married and started a family, and is now a stable and valuable member of his community. He is also pleased his life turned into something positive. He admits that while he was in India he prayed constantly for happiness, and he worked hard to free himself of his hatred and negativity. It took him a long time to find himself, but once he did he never looked back on his youth with anything but thanks that he had an opportunity to grow and develop. He could easily have remained a Victim of abusive parents but chose instead to find the courage to ask for more from life and to do the work that was required to make him positive and affirmative about life.

# *Functional Archetype: The Mother*

## Recognizing The Mother

As we complete the section on the Victim, we bring our attention to the positive archetype of the Root Chakra—the Mother. The Mother represents our ability to nourish and look after the life force within us with care, sensitivity and vigilance.

Of all the archetypes, the Mother is the one we understand the best. She is fundamental in our relationship with ourselves and with life. She is so deeply rooted in our being that it is impossible to detach ourselves from her influence in our lives. As we develop an understanding of ourselves as individuals we will also see the Mother archetype in a new light.

As we become whole within ourselves we learn to love and honor that part of ourselves the Mother represents. Integrating this archetype is essential to our development, for she teaches us how to take care of ourselves and to respect our needs. She helps us integrate the feminine aspects of our personality so that we can develop our capacity to love; love ourselves, love all people, love life. As we develop the Mother within ourselves we stop projecting our needs on to the world around us and integrate her into our lives so that we are able to look after ourselves.

When we are wounded, or abused in the process of living our lives, we can find the love within ourselves and call upon the Mother to help us heal. As we become grounded in the knowledge of what and who is good for us we start to differentiate the superficial and unsavory from what is truly good for us, what sustains us and what contributes to our happiness and well-being.

## *Our own good Mother*

The Mother archetype also assists us in healing the wounds from inadequate parenting and helps us find love within ourselves. If our own mother was unable to grow psychologically and spiritually to develop a life of her own we can help her by giving ourselves what we need. This makes our own lives richer and more fulfilling as we stop projecting our needs on to her, or substitutes for her, to look after us and make us *right*. As this archetype develops in us we become our own good Mothers.

Recently a friend of mine, pregnant for the first time, had to undergo surgical intervention which was life-saving for her unborn child. She worried about the effects the anesthesia would have on her child and spent several days beforehand talking to her child in meditation. She assured it that she was consciously choosing to have this operation for the baby's sake and that all would be well. She drew on her motherly instincts to soothe and care for her child. She integrated the primal Mother archetype within herself to assure her baby that they were both going to be safe.

When we are dependent on others to provide us with our nurturing we are not allowing our own Mother archetype to flourish. There are many adults emotionally arrested in childhood, who have yet to grow up and resource their own internal capacity to look after themselves. They still expect that someone will answer the deep needs of their undernourished self by taking over the role which was incomplete in their lives. Basically, the role of psychotherapy is to release the traumas and hurt created in our formative years. It helps everyone who is willing to delve into their family history to cleanse the pain and release the hurt of the past. It helps create a strong and viable Mother archetype.

### The Earth Mother

The Mother is deeply rooted in earth energy. As Earth Mother she provides the goodness and sustenance we need to thrive and grow. She looks after us, feeds us and is always able to provide for our needs. As with all mothers, we know that we can count on her.

We all carry the template of this archetype within us. When we are Victims, disconnected from the source of this energy, we lose our grounding, which is so deeply linked to the Mother archetype. As we look after ourselves and provide the fundamentals of care and nurturing we become more mature and able to meet life's challenges with clarity and focus. When we are our own good Mother we know our body's limitations, our emotional strength and fragility and our mental ability to think clearly. When we are our own good Mother we know where we stand in life, literally and figuratively.

Mothers are synonymous with life, and life becomes simple when we reconnect to our roots in the earth and the Mother archetype within. She helps us be well and feel safe. When things become complex or out of balance in our lives it is important to know how to mother ourselves. This may mean doing simple things which comfort and sustain us. For instance, whenever I feel unsettled or overwhelmed by change I enjoy cleaning my home, gardening or cooking. This is my way of keeping chaos away. A friend, during a difficult time in her life, enjoyed making soups. A man I know makes pieces of furniture, another one tinkers on his car for hours. These activities are grounding and simple and give comfort. Mothers know what heals and soothes. Tapping into this archetype allows us to be good Mothers to ourselves in ways which stabilize us. This way we light the flame of our own inner hearth and give ourselves the spiritual sustenance we need.

If we have ventured far from our roots the Mother archetype will be cut off from the vital supply of love and energy she needs to thrive. This can leave us confused and with a mistaken sense of identity. We can lose our ground of being and life can become chaotic, which drains and depletes our energy.

A function of the Mother archetype is to be aware of what is needed to keep balance and harmony in our lives and to see that we are nourished, well cared for and loved. As mothers are expected to tune into and respond to the needs of their child, we too are expected to tune into ourselves and listen to what we need in order to maintain harmony. The more we can draw upon this function of the Mother archetype the healthier we become. Loving and caring for ourselves then becomes natural.

# DEVELOPING THE MOTHER

## Taking Responsibility For Yourself

One of the ways to take responsibility for yourself is by looking after your needs. This means that you are capable of nurturing yourself and know what you need to feel safe and secure.

Being your own good Mother suggests that you are able to manage your life so that you can be healthy and happy. This means, at a practical level, that you eat well and take care of your physical needs. The better you are able to feed yourself, rest when you need it and give yourself comfort, the less dependent you are on others to mother you. You will learn to create a stable base within yourself from which to move out into the world; a safe haven within, free from interference, opposition or stress. Mothering and nourishing yourself means understanding what you need and letting yourself have it, to the best of your ability. This means knowing what to do, for example, when you are stressed and tired, and need to replenish your energy. It also means being discerning about how you spend your time and whom you choose as friends.

## Exercise

1 Recall an experience when you felt you were unable to look after yourself. For whatever reason, whether you were ill, tired or emotionally upset, you needed the help of someone else to regain your strength and stability. How did you feel about this situation? Did you feel better for someone else's care?

2 Can you remember how you got the support you needed to recuperate? Were you patient and understanding with yourself? Did your family or friends give you the support you needed? Was it their willingness to stick by you that helped you get better? Did you know that you had to look after yourself?

3 Can you give yourself time off from the stress and strain in your life now? Do you know when you need rest and relaxation? Do you know how to protect yourself from the pressures of work or relationships which are fraught?

4 Look at the people in your life now. Do you feel you could call on them to assist you when you are in need of help? Do you feel entitled to ask for help when you need it?

5 Are you willing to take responsibility for yourself to the best of your ability? Are you willing to look after your own physical and emotional needs?

6 Can you build in the care and nurturing you need for yourself in your life now? How can you change your life to include your needs in your daily routine?

Reflect on how you can best be your own good Mother.

## The Myth Of The Mother Archetype

Look at the myths which surround the Mother archetype and see if any of these themes correspond to your life. You have the ability to transform any ideas about yourself which do not enhance or support you.

Many people believe they need someone to look after them or do things for them in order to survive. They expect other people to be there for their needs and gratification, and they experience themselves as a helpless child in need of care.

As we mature we learn to become self sufficient, both physically and emotionally. This means the illusions we have about being mothered become redefined in terms of our ability to know what we need. If we are waiting for others to look after us, or to tell us what they think we need, we create a web of dependency which enmeshes us and suppresses our vital growth process. This denies us the pleasure of experiencing empowerment by being able to look after ourselves. Are you willing to examine your attitudes with regard to:

Nurturing?

Taking care of yourself?

Preparing your own food?

Cleaning your home?

Looking after your belongings?

Providing for your emotional needs?

Giving yourself the rest and relaxation you need?

Asking others for help?

Accepting the care and love others offer graciously without dependency?

Being able to separate yourself from highly dependent relationships which drain and deplete you?

With time and patience it is possible to create a healthy Mother archetype which serves all your needs. This archetype can sustain you and give you help to find your grounding so that you can create a healthy and happy life. It will help you to find the trust you need to thrive and look after yourself.

# MEDITATION

Sit in a comfortable position. Burn incense or aromatic oils if you like. As you take several deep breaths, begin to relax. Now visualize how you would feel if you could have all your physical and emotional needs met so that you felt contented and happy. See yourself as snug, happy and very safe.

Imagine that you are loved, happy and surrounded by the people you love the most, who contribute to your sense of well-being and belonging.

Take a deep breath and know that you are safe and secure. Feel that you are cherished and loved, and all is well in your world. Stop worrying about life and begin to trust that you are supported in positive, nourishing ways. Everything is taken care of, and you feel free of the burdens and worries that have made you unsure and uncertain about your future.

As you invest your energy into your healing, you are aware that you are maturing and developing into a person who can handle responsibility with both grace and grit. Enjoy the ease which comes from feeling this investment of love and energy into yourself. You are worth it. You can let go of the past and experience that you have a Mother within you which looks after your needs and desire. She helps you to stay grounded when you need to and she helps keep your life simple and easy. Trust her and appreciate that she is a growing part of you. As you respect and honor her within yourself she will look after and protect you.

Now visualize a color to soothe and heal your worries and anxieties. You can choose pink, which is the color of mother love, or choose another color which attracts you. Let it add to your growing sense of comfort and the protection you feel towards yourself. Enjoy the glow which comes from feeling happy with your life; free, even momentarily, from anxiety and stress.

## Vitality

This exercise opens the Root chakra and is designed to help you awaken your basic life force. At the most physical level it involves supporting the base of your spine and taking the tension off your lower back.

Begin by lying in a semi-supine position with a 3-inch book under the base of your skull and place your feet on the ground with your knees up. Let your hands rest on your pelvis with your elbows as far away from one another as possible. This stretches your spine and lengthens your back. If you can rest in this position for approximately 20 minutes you will release the tension of supporting your body all the time.

This exercise supports your back and allows you to let go of tension. Doing this daily, particularly after working hard, helps you feel better in yourself. It also grounds your energy in a very gentle and easy way. It enables you to experience yourself as lighter and removes blocks of tension in your back. This is an exercise in non-doing, and allows the body to rest and restore itself. It is a way of relaxing and, at the same time, it recharges your vitality. It allows you to take care of your body and also to feel good.

## Empowerment

Without a strong Mother archetype you will falter and stumble through life. This archetype is the foundation for your growth and development, and helps give you the awareness you need to take care of yourself. Say the following affirmations in the most loving and caring way you can, respecting that you are both the child and the mother.

I love and protect my inner child.

I take care of myself at all times.

I trust myself to know what is for my highest good and greatest joy.

I look after my needs in the best way I can.

I nourish my body, mind and spirit with love and tenderness.

I affirm that I am able to take responsibility for looking after myself in all ways.

I honor the Mother in me which knows what is best for me at all times.

I listen to myself and honor all my needs.

I trust that my needs can be met in a loving and respectful way.

I release all doubts and fears which block the way for love and abundance to come into my life.

I know that I am worth giving myself the things I need.

I take time to care for myself.


## Case Histories

### Bridget

Bridget is a successful business woman in her early forties. She is strong-willed and assertive, but has also suffered from bouts of depression. She felt a failure as a woman because she couldn't maintain an intimate relationship and she deeply longed to have children.

She worked in therapy for several years to ground her emotional energy and understand herself better. She became softer and more emotionally open to her feelings and her real self. She was able to experience her longing for love and emotional fulfillment.

At a certain point in her therapy she decided to take a holiday in the Mediterranean and planned to swim with dolphins. This experience completely changed her life. The sea is the mother of us all and she had the opportunity to reconnect with her Mother archetype. Through her experience with the dolphins she became clear that raising a child was essential to her. This longing was partly her way of healing the wounded child within her, and she felt prepared to take on the full responsibility by herself. She knew she had a large reserve of love to offer a child.

She returned from her holiday and made plans to sell her business, and she applied to adopt a child. Within months her life was transformed, and she became a joyful and radiant woman. She adopted a five-year-old Vietnamese girl and her life took on a totally new perspective. All the financial rewards and success she had accumulated in her work had never provided her with the level of happiness or satisfaction she gained in being a mother. She continued therapy to work through her emotional problems and to make sure she did not project them onto her child. She had clearly awakened the Mother archetype within herself which had laid dormant for many years and, in doing so, she was able to heal herself and give another Victim a chance for new life.

## *Jonathan*

Jonathan was 26 when circumstances forced him to acknowledge the Mother archetype in himself. His wife became very ill after their second child was born and she was unable to look after their children. He was forced to become both father and mother to his children. The younger child was only a few months old when he thought he might have to give up his job to look after the baby properly. Instead, he got permission to bring the baby into work where he looked after it. The women in his office helped him, as did his mother and several women friends. He struggled to manage his job, which required careful planning and pre-cision skills, and looking after the constant needs of his family. In the evening when he got home, instead of relaxing, he was forced to attend to organizing meals and seeing that the children were looked after before see-ing to his own needs. At times he felt he was two people trying to fulfill these roles. He also had the additional burden of his wife's illness.

He stayed grounded throughout the ordeal and always attended to what needed doing. At times when he was highly stressed he employed someone to look after the children so he could get out to the hills for a walk. He felt this helped him rebalance his energy and give him focus. This was his connection with Mother Earth.

His wife eventually recovered and resumed her function of looking after the children. His family is now thriving and his children have a spe-cial relationship with their dad. They love hearing the story about how he played mother to them for several months. At some unconscious level they know how deeply he cherishes them.

# 4

# THE SACRAL CHAKRA
## Pleasure, well-being, sexuality and abundance

DYSFUNCTIONAL ARCHETYPE:
*The Martyr*

FUNCTIONAL ARCHETYPE:
*The Empress/Emperor*

## HOW THE SACRAL CHAKRA FUNCTIONS

The Sacral chakra governs our sense of taste and appetite. This applies to the physical levels as well as the more spiritual sense of loving and enjoying life. Our well-being, our sense of sexuality and our permission to give ourselves prosperity and abundance are all focused in this chakra which is located in the center of our belly. It is through this chakra that our sense of boundary becomes developed and we are able to understand what will enhance and enrich our life. From this center we create life and move freely into the material world. The Sacral chakra is influenced by the element of water and as a result our emotions, which when fluid and moving keep us healthy, are related.

The archetypes of the Sacral chakra are the Martyr and the Empress/Emperor. They form the polarity of suffering and sacrifice on the one hand, and pleasure, happiness and contentment on the other. The Martyr archetype is unhappy and relinquishes responsibility for its well-being. The Empress/Emperor enjoys the abundance of life and looks for pleasure in everything. The Martyr disowns its entitlement to fulfillment and lets its energy dissipate by always seeking approval and helping others. The Empress/Emperor, on the other hand, enjoys itself and always has a good time, whatever it does. It enjoys everything in life. All things serve to enhance this archetype's love of pleasure and well-being. The Martyr struggles to have enough energy or enough money and is often depleted and exhausted, while the Empress/Emperor is overflowing with an abundance of energy for the activities it loves to do.

## *Dysfunctional Archetype: The Martyr*

### Recognizing The Martyr

The Martyr archetype does take a greater degree of responsibility for itself than the Victim, but it is not strong enough in its sense of self to be empowered or vitalized.

The Martyr's life is full of suffering. It is unable to make the necessary changes to shift its negative attitudes and its energy is often stale and stagnant. The Martyr suffers over the many things that happen in the course of life. Whatever the situation, the Martyr is unable to liberate its heavily negative attitudes towards life and create the joy and happiness it so desperately desires.

This archetype feels helpless to do anything to change its situation. It stays enmeshed and involved in situations which deplete its well-being, and often suffers for the sake of others. It does not feel entitled to personal happiness and can suffer for years, unable to change its life patterns. The Martyr relinquishes its claim to happiness in order to maintain peace, stability and balance for others. This can be at the detriment of its own mental and emotional health and physical well-being.

Many times the Martyr feels it is doing the right thing for children, spouse or parents by living an incomplete and unfulfilled life, and suffering at the expense of its own creativity and personal well-being. It feels the situation is hopeless or can't be changed. It is tragic to watch the Martyr's personal happiness drain away with every denial of true self. This can make it embittered and angry when those it sacrifices itself for leave or pass away.

Sacrifice best describes the nature of this archetype. There is also a deep sense of guilt about it as the Martyr feels it deserves the suffering it has imposed on itself.

## Collusion with the Martyr

It is, in many ways, more difficult to treat a Martyr in a therapeutic situation than a Victim. This is because our culture validates sacrifice and sometimes encourages people to give up their dreams for the sake of others. Nothing will disempower a person quicker than feeling they must give up their dreams for someone else's happiness. Whether it is done for approval or because of a desire to be loved and looked after, it diminishes a person when they do not choose to live their own lives.

Many people collude with the Martyr to carry on suffering rather than to take the risks which will transform its life. Families and friends unconsciously encourage the Martyr to continue its tasks of looking after others so that they are free of the responsibility of having to do it.

While the Victim knows it must do something to change its situation, the Martyr can endure for years without making fundamental changes in its life. It blocks its life force, creates co-dependent relationships and never seems to really enjoy itself.

The Martyr accepts a situation without making the changes which will empower it or give it more of a claim to happiness. It does, however, receive appreciation from others who share the same attitudes about suffering being a good thing. This, in the end, is its only reward.

This insidious pattern gets passed down to the Martyr's children or other people it is close to. Resentment runs deep, as blame and guilt are acted out in a punishing and nasty cycle. No one likes to feel others have sacrificed for them or that they are indebted and must sacrifice in return. The Martyr has the ability to make others feel guilty when they express their feelings about what they wish to do. It is as though others have done something wrong by openly expressing their feelings or desires, exactly what the Martyr would never do.

The Martyr gives up responsibility for its well-being and expects others to do the same. Its strength and power lie in manipulating others to do as it does. This is, in effect, how it controls others and appears to be right. The Martyr learns early in life to sacrifice itself by trying to win the love it was not receiving. This, of course, sets the pattern for life and only through consciously seeing that it has neither happiness nor vitality is it willing to start making the changes it needs to make its life work. The underlying theme with the Martyr is that it doesn't feel worthy of receiving love. It aids and abets its own devaluation by re-enforcing patterns of behavior which negate its growth and happiness.

*Making a step towards empowerment*

When we acknowledge that it is our right to have a choice to be and do what we want, then we are making a step towards our empowerment. The Martyr archetype can be shifted. It takes a willingness to look deeply at the emotional issues which block its happiness. We all have patterns of martyrdom in our families. It could come in the form of a parent, aunt or cousin who gave up an opportunity for growth and change. When we accept the Martyr's attitude we collude in saying that life isn't good or worth the risk of change. The reason the Martyr doesn't change is that its suffering is a way of making it special. The choice to be happy is available to us all when we choose to release this archetype from our consciousness. We open the path to pleasure and happiness when we let go of our suffering and pain.

# MOVING ON FROM THE MARTYR

## Taking Responsibility For Yourself

The position of the Martyr can be stuck and entrenched. This is because the Martyr truly believes it is doing the right thing for itself even at the expense of its aliveness and well-being. It thinks sacrifice is good for the self. This leaves a large residue of anger and resentment for everyone to deal with and invites contempt and difficulties. Through sacrifice the Martyr hides its inability or unwillingness to develop its life. It gets caught in rescuing and fixing other people's lives, often giving up its own creativity, sexuality and health to do this. Perhaps worst of all, the Martyr expects sacrifice in return from others as acceptable behavior, when in fact sacrifice erodes people's potential for a rich and fulfilling life.

## Exercise

1 Recall a situation when you were aware of being a Martyr. This may have occurred in your work, your personal life or with people you were close to. The criterion for this is that you experienced sacrificing yourself for someone else.

**2** What are your feelings about this situation now? Can you recall what your expectations were for yourself and what you hoped sacrifice would bring you? Were you looking for love or approval?

**3** Look at the situation where you experienced being a Martyr and ask yourself if you harbor resentment for not having your sacrifice recognized. What are your feelings? Be willing to be honest with yourself so that you can release your negativity about this situation and let it go.

**4** Are you willing to take responsibility for this situation without falling into guilt or self-recrimination? If you can see it for what it is you may avoid falling into this pattern again.

**5** Can you accept your need for love and appreciation? Can you accept that your willingness to sacrifice yourself was an attempt to win love and approval from others? Can you accept that you needn't sacrifice yourself to be loved? Love belongs to you simply because you exist. If this is too difficult for you to accept give some thought to your feelings of entitlement to love and happiness.

## The Myth Of The Martyr Archetype

As you read about the myths that Martyrs fabricate their lives around, ask yourself if this is how you want to live your life. What are you willing to do in the present moment to bring happiness and joy into your life? The point of power is within you and the moment to begin is now! Only you have the personal power to divest the myth of any hold over you. As you release the energy invested in this myth, you will become lighter, freer and more able to enjoy the goodness in life.

The myth of the Martyr is a difficult one to transform in our society for, as we have seen, there is a myth that sacrifice is good for us. Many people would rather sacrifice for a worthy cause or a difficult situation than look inside at the emptiness of their own lives and the myths which stop them from growing. The real truth is that no one enjoys a sufferer. They drain our energy and exasperate our goodwill. Compassion is something we should all develop but it isn't the same as pity. Pity is what the Martyr evokes in us. We say: "Oh, poor so and so, how they suffer." This doesn't give anyone the energy they need to move on to develop a happy life. Compassion, on the other hand, recognizes that someone is having a difficult time and we can be sincerely sorry for their suffering. We don't try to change their situation or take it away from them, nor do we ignore their pain.

If you are willing to look at the myths which run your life ask yourself some of the following questions.

Do you think it is better to give than receive?

Do you feel that you are less worthy than someone else to receive good things?

How do you feel about your entitlement to happiness? Do you feel that you are worthy of it?

Do you feel that you are worthy of receiving the things you want in life? Do you feel you have to sacrifice to receive them or give your life up in some way?

Are you willing to put up with a chronically bad situation without making changes to facilitate your freedom and joy?

Are you willing to develop your creativity and live your own life?

What is it you really want which will bring you happiness and joy?

## MEDITATION

Sit or lie in a position where you are comfortable. Burn some incense if you wish and begin to relax. Take several deep breaths in through your nose and out through your mouth.

As you relax visualize a situation where you felt you were sacrificing your aliveness and creativity. Hold the image of this situation in your mind, and begin to release your anger and resentment around it. You may say words like: "I am angry at you for not recognizing my needs".

Repeat these words until you feel that you have been heard. Now imagine that you are recognized for all that you have done. Imagine that you are being told: "I/We recognize your needs and release you to do what you need to do for yourself." Repeat this to yourself.

As you come back to yourself release this image and let it go. You may want to do this again with other situations where you have felt like a Martyr.

At the end of each scene visualize a healing color surrounding you. See this color enveloping you and let it act as a healing light to soothe away your emotional pain. Allow yourself to recognize your need to be loved and embrace that need with your own love.

Let that love grow and mature in yourself.

Use this meditation for any other situations where you have felt like a Martyr.

## Vitality

As you begin to draw your energy back into yourself and withdraw your projections from others you begin to regain your love for yourself. You may experience bursts of energy being released throughout your body. One of the most basic ways of not being a Martyr is to do things you really enjoy. Eliminate sacrifice from your life as much as you can.

Sit quietly and listen to your inner voice. Let it guide you to do things that let you express your vitality and joy. These may be very simple things like the following.

Painting a picture

Visiting a friend

Talking on the phone

Buying a magazine

Writing a poem

Starting a journal

Playing with a pet

Replanting your house plants

Playing music and dancing

Going shopping

For further inspiration look at the Vitality list for the Victim on page 38.

Whenever you do things you enjoy you are revitalizing your energy. The more you can do the things which give you pleasure the more you step out of the Martyr archetype.

## Empowerment

Do these affirmations with the awareness that you always have a choice. If you are in a situation where you feel like a Martyr remember the focus of power is always in the present moment and you can choose to sacrifice yourself or stand up for what you feel is the best for you. Open your mind and heart to the following affirmations.

*I release sacrifice from my life. I do what I choose for my own well-being and happiness.*

*I am a free agent at all times and can fully communicate my feelings about any situation I am in.*

*I release the doubts and fears which hold me back from experiencing the love I know I deserve.*

*I choose to love myself unconditionally at all times.*

*I am entitled to happiness, health and joy in my life.*

*I forgive the past and embrace myself fully.*

*I take the steps I need to grow so that I am able to fulfil myself in the best ways possible.*

*I am capable of releasing myself from any situation which doesn't let me be fully the person I am.*

*I acknowledge my mistakes and reaffirm my self-esteem. I deserve the best for my life.*

*I am thankful for the learning experience which comes from making mistakes. I am a quick learner and will do what is best for me in the future.*

*I am capable of healing my life. I choose to seek assistance and help where I feel it will benefit my awareness and growth.*

*No one needs to fix me or heal me. I reclaim my power to look after myself. I deserve happiness and joy.*

## Case Histories

### Sybil

Sybil was unhappily married. In her mid-thirties, she was childless and in stable, but non-sexual, marriage. Her husband was a successful business man and they enjoyed a comfortable life. When she came to me for consultation, she said her problem was that she felt guilty about her sexuality, and sought refuge in spiritual causes which put her out of her body and away from her feelings. She was a member of a spiritual circle which believed in celibacy and this gave her the cover she needed to not have to confront her discomfort about sexuality. She displaced nearly all her emotional energy in her spiritual practices. She could meditate for hours, chant, and go to group meetings where people idolized their guru and invested their life with purpose through their devotion to him.

Sybil appeared absent most of the time, with a vacant look in her eyes, and she was difficult to make contact with. She was not in touch with herself or the world around her.

As we started to explore her archetypes and the myths which ran her life, she confessed that sexuality had been a big taboo in her family when she was a child. She was terrified of her passion and longings. Her mother had had several children, but told her daughter constantly that she hated sex. Her mother was a typical Martyr and her daughter was beginning to follow in her footsteps.

Over time, and with considerable work on herself, she began to let go of the negative attitudes and fears which blocked her awareness of her body. She became more responsive to her environment, both emotionally and physically, and she spent more time together with her husband. She began to openly discuss her desire and longing to enjoy sex with him.

Eventually she did achieve what she wanted. She created both a healthy sexual and emotional relationship with her partner, and became an empowered woman who could express her needs and feelings. She took the best from her spiritual practice and left what didn't work for her. She is now a fulfilled person, having left behind her suffering Martyr archetype.

## Jake

Jake is a handsome man in his early thirties. He came to see me for a health problem which seemed unrelated to his emotional life, or so it appeared at the time. When we started to talk, it became clear he was in a very unhappy relationship with a woman who had his child. He and the woman lived separately in the same house, and only communicated with one another when necessary. They went on vacations together with their young daughter and made every attempt to appear to be a family. He deeply loved and cared for his child, and felt if he stayed in the house and saw her every day she would benefit from this arrangement.

The more he maintained this idea of sacrificing his life for his child the worse his physical symptoms became. He developed migraine headaches and odd rashes and aches which debilitated him and often brought him to the brink of self pity. He had not developed any nurturing friendships which would have helped sustain him through this difficult living arrangement, and he felt very isolated and alone with his choice. He had little support and open hostility from the mother of his child. She treated him with contempt and disdain, and was openly offensive to him in front of the child.

As we worked together over the months, a few important facts about his life became apparent. His own father had died when he was young and this left a hole in his life which was never filled. He transposed his own

enjoyed. It is sociable and loves parties and gatherings with friends and family. It never deprives itself or withholds pleasure from itself. It allows itself the spirit of abundance in whatever it does. It looks after its health, gets enough rest, food and exercise and is never short of affection or touch. Its joy for life pervades everything.

This archetype does not have a deeply developed inner world; things tend to be manifested in the physical world. It is engaged with the bounty of life, often without an awareness of the spiritual source which sustains it, but it is a very happy and alive archetype.

# DEVELOPING THE EMPRESS/EMPEROR

## Taking Responsibility For Yourself

The level of awareness this archetype has is linked with the material world and the high levels of creative energy which are necessary to maintain a happy and healthy lifestyle. Though this is an important stage of life there is more to personal development and growth than pleasure and an easy life. We have increasingly more pathways to healing and growth available to us when we are open to living in the emotional and spiritual realms of life. It helps us to love life fully and express our feelings when we detach our identity from what we have and what we do. Then we can start to recognize our inner nature as well.

## Exercise

1 Recall an experience when you felt that life was *on your side*, and you felt supported and happy with yourself. Try to remember what it felt like when life was going your way and savor the memory of that, however brief it was for you. Stay focused on what was good and felt joyful to you. If you have no memory of this in your life fantasize a scene where you experience feeling that life could be on your side and imagine it the way you would like it to be.

2 How do you feel about this scenario? Do you feel that you are worthy of more moments like this? Does well-being feel natural and easy to you? Can you be comfortable with it?

**3** Look at the people and situation in your experience or vision. What do you experience when you see this positive image? Is it trust, gratitude, pleasure or a combination of these qualities which make your life feel positive and good?

**4** Are you willing to take responsibility for your ability to create a warm and positive environment for yourself? Do you wish to create more times when you feel happy and well in yourself? Open your imagination and create several beautiful images of your future in your mind. It is from instilling sensations and feelings with positive images that you can create the future. You can make the joy and happiness you deserve by thinking positively about what you want.

## The Myth Of The Empress/Emperor Archetype

The myths attached to this archetype are particularly relevant to our western culture at this time. Although this is a happy and positive archetype, there is still so much within us that can be developed. As you look at the myths associated with the Empress/Emperor, let go of any fixed ideas you may have about want and desire. The more you suppress your desires, the more they can twist themselves in your mind until what you thought you wanted becomes mixed with your need for love, friendship, independence and prosperity.

Many of us have been brought up with the myth that our value as people is dependent on what we do and what we have. We are measured by the car we drive, the clothes we wear, the job status we have and how attractive our partner is. But these things are not who we are, they are only what we have. We are limited to a temporal and material existence if we define ourselves by these values alone.

What would happen, for instance, if you lost your money, split up with your partner and got fired from your job? Would you be less lovable, less worthy of kindness and respect without these things? Give some thought to what you would be like if you were suddenly stripped of all these external things and you were left without the trappings of your life. Can you find the depth of love and approval for yourself that you need without these things that define your life? Can you love yourself simply for who you are?

This over-identification with material well-being is not who we are. Our sensitivity and spiritual awareness are measured by the depth of our ability to experience life with joy and to take responsibility for expressing ourselves to our fullest, no matter where we are or what we have. Though it is pleasurable to have possessions which reflect our capacity to earn a living they shouldn't be confused with our personal identity. Look at the myths in your life surrounding material possessions. Are you valued for what you have or what you do rather than who you are? Would you forsake your dreams or your creativity for material comfort?

Are you willing to release the myths that limit your self approval to what you possess and what you do? See if you can expand your love for yourself to include a deeper and richer sense of who you are. The good feelings which come from loving yourself are not dependent upon anything material in your life. These feelings come from being deeply connected to the Source within you. This gives you the space to be in the world and enjoy its pleasures, but not overly identified with it.

## MEDITATION

Sit comfortably and take a few deep breaths. Burn incense and a candle. Hold a mirror in front of your eyes and look deeply into it. Take in your own beauty. Look at yourself for a few moments and begin to open yourself to the love and approval you so eagerly desire. Give it to yourself now. Graciously love yourself as you look into your eyes and say to yourself:

*Hello. I love you. I honor you and I recognize your needs.*

*I am creating the very best for you that I know how. I care for you.*

*I listen to you and I love you unconditionally. You don't have to do anything or be anything other than who you are for me to love you.*

When you have given yourself this love close your eyes and feel the radiance and peace of that love moving through you as you sit quietly in meditation. Allow these feelings to give you a sense of well-being and joy.

Choose a color which expresses the warmth you feel for yourself and let it surround you as you bask in the light of your own love.

## Vitality

To increase the energy in your Sacral chakra create a moving meditation for yourself which combines movement and conscious thought. This is what happens in martial arts which are focused in this center. You can increase your vitality with any form of movement where you are aware of your self and what you are doing. Here are some examples.

Try swimming and holding an affirmation in your mind while you glide through the water.

Walk in nature and empty your mind of all thoughts so that you can experience being in the present moment.

Do the same while cycling, skating, skiing, or playing tennis or squash.

The aim is that as you bring your awareness into the present moment and open yourself to the goodness and joy that is within you, you can move more freely and easily. As you do this more and more energy will move through you.

## Empowerment

As you do the following affirmations say them in the present moment. Allow yourself to feel how good it is to say positive things about yourself. Feel how stabilizing it can be to trust yourself.

*I am beautiful and everyone loves me.*

*I am happy and content at all times. Nothing can ruffle my feathers unless I let it.*

*I am powerful and influential in my world.*

*I enjoy my body and feel good about my sexuality.*

*I feel happy with myself.*

*I love who I am.*

*Life is sweet and I enjoy it.*

*I am enough and what I do is enough.*

*I am prosperous and love having money. I love money and money loves me.*

*I take good care of myself and feel comfortable wherever I am.*

*Life feels good right now.*

*I give myself permission to fully enjoy everything I do.*

*I share my warmth and joy.*

*I am easy with myself and trust my life is unfolding in wonderful and joyful ways.*

*I accept pleasure as a part of my being.*

*I enjoy being free and open to the goodness around me.*

## Case Histories

### Deirdre

Deirdre lived in Europe. She had a strong desire to develop her intuition and psychic abilities. When I met her she was in her early forties and had three children from a former marriage. She ran a psychological center for creative development. Her energy was strongly focused in the Sacral chakra and her archetype was definitely the Empress. She made sure everything in her life worked well and was in plentiful supply. She was proud of her home and her material wealth. She worked hard to maintain her home and she had several business investments which brought her sufficient income so that she could choose what she wanted to do with her time.

She wore beautiful and expensive clothing, and she loved treating herself to small gifts whenever possible. She also enjoyed cooking and gardening. Her life was geared to give her the maximum pleasure. She enjoyed being massaged, and any form of treatment which helped her relax and feel good about herself was patronized.

However, something was lacking in her development. She was intent on showing others that she possessed psychic powers and could channel spiritual energy to help them. She worked hard to rise above her comfort zone and, finally, after a struggle, managed to unlock psychic gifts.

As she opened up to the higher realms of channeling she admitted she had been a very poor child and had nearly starved at the end of the World War II. Material comfort had been important to her and nearly stopped her from developing her spiritual gifts. Material wealth was a touchstone of her well-being and gave her the sense that she was fine.

Soon after she opened her spiritual awareness, she began a relationship with a wealthy man who provided her with the emotional security she had longed for. She was then able to devote herself entirely to working with people to help them open to their spirituality. As she let go of trying to be the Empress archetype, she was truly able to be that gracious person she wanted to be, and in doing so reached a higher level of personal development.

## *Jacob*

Jacob is a good example of the Emperor archetype. He is in his early sixties and worked for many years to establish a career working for a large corporation. He had a good marriage and four children. He lived in a beautiful part of Britain in a lovely and spacious home. He took trips abroad, drank good French wine, went to the theater, opera and concerts. He was a rugged sportsman, and loved mountaineering and sailing. He lived from his Sacral chakra center, and was stable, steady and reliable, as this archetype generally is. When his life went through upheaval at one point, he was hard pressed to leave his comfort zone. He lost both his parents within a short time, as well as his job, which he had been in for 20 years, and around this time his wife asked for a divorce to go and pursue a career.

With so many changes, all he wanted to do was stay rooted in his past. It bothered him that he was unable to maintain the status quo in his life. It took him a few years to make the shifts in his thinking and to know what he wanted to do. He maintained many of the pleasures he had always enjoyed and took up several new interests as well.

He developed a new line of business which he found rewarding and challenging, and over a period of time he managed to step on to higher ground. Throughout these changes his basic integrity never faltered nor his belief in the goodness of his life.

One of the things that he maintained was the quality of life he had always had, though he scaled it down to fit a single person. At the same time he expanded his creativity through new work, and he embarked on a loving and supportive relationship with a woman who shared many of his interests. This enabled him to manifest his Emperor archetype to its full extent.

Through the changes he was forced to undergo, he could easily have become one of life's victims and been unable to make the necessary changes in his thinking. He never lost his basic faith and trust in life, and this was the foundation upon which he continues to grow.

# 5

# THE SOLAR PLEXUS CHAKRA

Self-esteem, self-worth, confidence,
decision-making and personal power

DYSFUNCTIONAL ARCHETYPE:
*The Servant*

FUNCTIONAL ARCHETYPE:
*The Warrior*

## HOW THE SOLAR PLEXUS CHAKRA FUNCTIONS

The Solar Plexus chakra is intrinsically linked with our sense of self-worth and personal power. Its energy helps us to feel self-respecting, decisive and confident. When we are submissive or susceptible to the influences of other people, the energy from this center becomes weak and we find ourselves disempowered.

The Solar Plexus is an important chakra because it controls the intake and outflow of energy which is generated in our interchanges with others. This allows us to deal with people on both an emotional and an instinctual level. When this center is in balance it gives us satisfying and healthy relationships because we are relating from a strong sense of who we are. When we own our power and accept our value, knowing that we truly deserve the very best for ourselves, we invite people to show us care, kindness and respect. When we have owned our power we can then move on to higher levels of empowerment and deeper bonds of love.

When we fail to value and honor ourselves we find we take the brunt of other people's negativity and sometimes find ourselves poorly treated. When this center is weak we can create experiences which undermine our self-worth and diminish our confidence.

The Solar Plexus focuses mainly on relationship issues. Our level of self-worth and self-respect gives our relationships quality and permits an equal exchange of emotional energy. We do not think or act in an inferior or superior way to others, we negotiate our relationships from a place of equality and we attract people who reflect our state of self-love and worth back to us in the most healthy and respectful way.

When we connect the Solar Plexus with the spiritual energy of the Crown chakra we put our relationships into a spiritual context in which they can unfold. This gives us a strong and ordered sense of life that supports peace of mind, personal integrity and an ability to transcend emotional conflicts.

The two archetypes representing the dysfunctional and functional aspects of this chakra are the Servant and the Warrior. They are polar opposites and reflect the ways in which we manifest self-worth and personal power in our lives.

## *Dysfunctional Archetype: The Servant*

### Recognizing The Servant

The Servant archetype undervalues itself and does not honor its basic worth. The Servant is not as dysfunctional or disempowered as the Victim or the Martyr, but it represents, rather, someone who does a job well but who is neglected and receives little acknowledgement for what it does. It is not a negative archetype, but the servant is not rewarded appropriately for all it does.

The Servant doesn't have a sense that it deserves better than what it receives in its life. It is thankful for whatever attention or acknowledgement it gets, whereas in healthy relationships everyone is acknowledged for what they contribute.

Acknowledgement is power. It frees people and as the Servant is ignored, it finds itself lingering in the background, never moving on to higher levels of achievement or empowerment. The Servant does not have enough of a sense of its esteem and worth to acknowledge itself and so is dependent on others to give it what it cannot give to itself. People take on the Servant archetype because they don't feel they are worth anything. This archetype relinquishes its personal power and emotional needs in order to win acknowledgement and approval. It projects its power on to others and makes them much more powerful than it is, investing them with qualities it would like to express but wouldn't dare.

### Beginning to change the Servant mentality

If we are dependent for acknowledgement from others for the jobs we do or the help we give, then we are linked with the Servant archetype. When we find ourselves longing for acknowledgement from others it becomes essential that we learn how to acknowledge ourselves. This is how we empower ourselves and move on from the Servant archetype.

Often, this archetype asks for love or recognition from the very people who are least capable or willing to give it. When this happens the Servant needs to give itself a realistic evaluation of its abilities and empower itself. At this point it needs to detach itself from the situation or person with whom it is emotionally entangled, release its projections of power into the other person and own its worth. If other people cannot recognize its value it may need to consider the importance of acknowledgement in its life and why it has put itself in a situation where it is not receiving what it wants. Personal power is not an area in which to be blocked because there are so many other levels of awareness that are more pleasurable and important for our self-development.

When the Servant lives for acknowledgement and recognition from others it is dependent on them for its well-being and it makes them responsible for its happiness. Thus it stays submissive and dependent on others. The Servant needs to know the simple truth that it doesn't need to do or be anything in order to be loved. It deserves love and consideration simply because it is worthy of it. Its value is not tied to what it does but to who it is.

The Servant always maintains a low profile. It is self-effacing and knows its place. At one level this reflects its understanding of its function and at another it is an expression of its submissiveness and the feeling that it is less worthy than someone else.

The Servant's ego is not well anchored in itself and its boundaries are easily invaded. This means it can be easily manipulated. There is difficulty distinguishing one's self from another. If the Servant defines itself through other's recognition of it then its sense of self needs to be strengthened. This comes in making choices which will reflect a deepening sense of self-worth and confidence and knowing that what one is good at in life is empowering.

The Servant seldom desires high levels of personal power and shuns the limelight. It can often suffer with diseases affecting the Solar Plexus area such as ulcers, digestive difficulties and migraine headaches. It is prone to nervous diseases and its physical vitality is often erratic. This is because in giving away its power, the Servant diminishes its vitality levels. The way this archetype can grow is by achieving personal empowerment through making healthy choices and strong commitments. It needs to make decisions for itself which focus on its well-being and its need for respect as well as acknowledgement from others. It is essential for its self-worth that the Servant knows its own sense of value.

### *Examples of the Servant archetype*

This archetype can be found in relationships where one partner thinks they are more important than the other. Everything revolves around one partner's needs and demands. The family supports the self importance of one person at the expense of other members of the family. There is a tacit agreement that this person's needs are more important and, as a consequence of this belief, everything revolves around them.

As members of the family give up their power to support this false image, they lose their self-esteem and sense of worth. Their real needs are neglected and they feel they don't count, first in the family context and, later, in life. Yet, it is often their support which makes it possible for this dynamic to occur in the first place.

Many wives find themselves in this secondary, Servant role where they are doing the supporting and are only acknowledged in terms of how well they do their job of supporting their husband and children. This role is also fulfilled by secretaries, nurses and other auxiliary helpers. There is nothing intrinsically the matter with these roles so long as people are able to receive the recognition they rightfully deserve.

This archetype is not gender related. Men who are the sons of domineering fathers often find later on that they work for bosses who are dictatorial and seldom give them acknowledgement.

# MOVING ON FROM THE SERVANT

## Taking Responsibility For Yourself

Taking responsibility for the Servant archetype is important for your self-esteem. By acknowledging that it may be easier for you to serve others than to take responsibility for what you want in your life is a real step towards your empowerment. You may find it difficult to recognize what you want for yourself or where your needs for recognition and acknowledgement stem from. If you were not recognized as a child it is possible you are still seeking that from your intimate relationships, your friends or your work situation.

If you feel that you have relinquished your right to make your own decisions about your life or enhance your personal power in a significant way, it is important that you take responsibility for your life now. You can begin by valuing yourself. The point of change and transformation is always in the present moment. Ask yourself if you are willing to be empowered by taking responsibility for your life and what you want. Acknowledging yourself for this decision is a step towards empowerment.

## Exercise

Remember a time when you lived out the Servant archetype either in a work situation or a personal relationship. How did you give away your power? Did that happen because you didn't feel worthy or because you felt someone else was more important than you? Could this have happened because you wanted to feel that you were good and you wanted others to acknowledge you? It is essential, if you wish to empower yourself, to acknowledge your own feelings about wanting to know if you are good enough.
Try asking yourself the following questions.

1 What did you gain from being subservient to someone else?

2 Did you get what you wanted from this person?

3 Do you believe that someone else deserves more or is more worthy of love and respect than you are?

**4** How do you feel about this situation now?

As you look at the situation in your mind's eye ask this person if they would be willing to acknowledge you now. If you receive a YES response than thank them and agree that you are worthy of it. If you get a NO, thank them anyway and acknowledge yourself for having done a wonderful job of supporting and helping them to the best of your ability. It is important that you know you are worthy of your own love and respect. Then you can forgive those who did not acknowledge you and let go of any shame or blame that is still attached to this situation. Release yourself from all the negativity surrounding this situation and be free.

## The Myth Of The Servant Archetype

So many people believe the myth that they are not worthy of the things they want. They often attract situations which mirror their worst feelings about themselves. This, if not consciously altered, will continually diminish their self esteem and erode their confidence. They may find themselves in situations or relationships where they are hoping for acknowledgement or approval from others and it is not forthcoming.

They may go on chasing this myth thinking the love or approval they want is just around the corner, and that all they have to do is change something or be better at something and the love and acknowledgement they seek will be theirs. This both undermines the self and is confidence-destroying to anyone who engages in a relationship with this attitude.

In truth, love and approval never come until we give them to ourselves. When we begin to value and honor who we are then we are on the road to empowerment. Validating ourselves will draw healthy and fulfilling experiences to us which reinforce our self-esteem and increase our confidence. When this happens we are less likely to find ourselves in abusive or unhappy situations. We avoid being involved with people who don't value who we are.

The myth of not being worthy can easily be perpetuated by people we are involved with in our families, churches and schools. You always need to ask yourself: "Am I receiving the love and respect I feel I deserve?" Are you willing to release the negative attitudes about your worth that block the love and joy you want? You don't have to suffer or struggle to be happy with yourself. It is important to believe that it is all available to you when you love and honor yourself.

As you examine the myths of the Servant, try to be aware that every experience in your life offers you the opportunity to learn more about who you are. Sometimes it is the *negative* experience which brings enlightenment. Often the petty tyrants of your life—whether they take the form of an overpowering parent, a nasty boss or an ungrateful lover—give you the chance to grow and expand your sense of worth. When you emerge from the struggle you are stronger, quickened and much less likely to be caught in relationships and situations which are not joyful and healthy.

# MEDITATION

Sit comfortably and relax. Take several deep breaths in through your nose and out through your mouth. Burn a candle or light incense if you like to keep the energy around you purified.

As you relax imagine you are walking along a beautiful path which leads up a high mountain. You want to go to the top of the mountain to meet an ancient sage who lives there. As you scramble over large boulders with precipitous drops, you are panting and out of breath. When you arrive at a shrine there is a very old man there sitting deep in meditation. You sit quietly in front of him and wait for him to recognize your presence. You go deeper into a relaxed state and before you are aware of it you are looking deeply inside yourself. When you open your eyes you realize that you are alone in this shrine. Suddenly you are aware that you are the sage whom you sought and you realize that all the answers you seek are inside yourself.

You no longer need to look for answers outside your self. Everything you need to know, however big or small, is within you. You offer thanks and come down the mountain, back into the world. You start your life with a new and deeper awareness of yourself.

Enjoy the feeling that you know your worth and that you deserve the very best of all things. Your work and your relationships are deeply satisfying and support you in being the best that you can be.

## Vitality

In order to increase your vitality and energize your Solar Plexus you may want to do some brave and courageous things which you haven't allowed yourself to do in the past. Consider what sort of activities would be appropriate for you and help you develop the inner skills to give you a deep sense that you are in command of your life. The following list of activities will help you.

Take a trip somewhere you haven't been on your own. Enjoy exploring and getting to know what is interesting and what this place evokes in you

Climb a mountain

Try a sport that is new and adventurous

Start a course of study of something you have always wanted to know more about

Sell or give away things that don't hold any more allure for you

Talk to someone who frightened you in the past

Talk to a friend or healer who can help you resolve issues about your life which block your happiness and health

Make some decisions about your life which involve going for what you want

## Empowerment

You can write down or speak these affirmations out loud. They can be said in front of a mirror or to yourself while you are swimming, driving or cooking a meal. They are designed to help you empower yourself.

*I love myself. I love myself. I love myself.*

*I am worthy of my own self acceptance.*

*I value who I am.*

*I cherish my sweetness and kind nature.*

*I value myself and I know what is best for me.*

*I know I am becoming the best possible person that I can be.*

*I champion my growing sense of self.*

*I accept responsibility for all decisions I make in my life.*

*I honor myself and treat myself with respect.*

*I have the power to remove myself from all abusive and negative situations which harm me.*

*I am the prime decision maker in my life.*

*As I own my power I recognize the strength and beauty of who I am.*

*I am worth all the good and the wonderful things I want.*

*I heal and grow every day.*

*I allow myself to become stronger and more alive each day.*

*As I build a strong and resilient ego I love and cherish all aspects of myself.*

*I refuse to let other people project their negativity into me. I am my own person, free to choose what is best for me.*

## Case Histories

### Rose

Rose is in her mid-forties and has been married for over 20 years to a wealthy doctor. She began therapy two years ago. She was a university graduate but decided to marry and start a family rather than face the challenges of a career. She had five children and has spent the rest of her married life looking after her home. As her children became older they grew accustomed to material comforts and luxury. Their father, who was busy with work, gave them gifts as a way of replacing quality time and attention. They drove fast cars, had expensive clothes and equipment, and went to private schools. They went on expensive summer and winter vacations.

Rose, when I met her, rode a bicycle. She wore old and well-worn clothes, and hadn't bought herself anything new in years. She looked ten years older than her age and she sported a black eye at our first appointment which was from an altercation with her husband. She had told him she was unhappy about her life. He wanted to know why she was so unappreciative of all the good things she had and he hit her in a fit of rage. He continued to abuse her for a long while into her treatment sessions. He could not abide her having feelings which did not fit his view of how he felt she should be. He was amazed that she could be unhappy and always reacted when she spoke up for herself.

It took a lot of work for Rose to develop her self-esteem. She had to learn to stand up for herself and feel that she counted. She was a bright and creative woman who had willingly sacrificed her life for others with little or no reward or recognition. She started making demands on her husband and threatening to withhold her support in the family structure. Life began to change quickly around her home. She left briefly for a vacation with a woman friend and the entire household ceased functioning. The family found it difficult to carry on without her, and when she returned they were kinder and more respectful.

Her struggle to speak up for herself has not been easy. She has no models in her family or among her close friends for this, or for developing her personal identity. She felt that she didn't count and she struggles with developing a sense of worth. She had been educated by nuns and was taught that a woman's place was to serve without the right to make demands.

Although it is a struggle for her, she is learning to love herself and to know she does makes a difference to others. Every day is a step away from the Servant archetype and into a more empowered archetype. As she values herself more deeply, her husband has begun to listen to her, and both he and her children are becoming more appreciative of her.

## *George*

George is in his late thirties and is a social worker. He is involved in a relationship with a woman who has his child. They live separately and he pays child support and visits his son on weekends, and the three of them go on vacations.

He and his son's mother are on friendly terms but they are no longer lovers. He complains about her often and her inability to be a nurturing parent to his son. As the years have unfolded, he has found himself bound up in this relationship where he is catering to both his son and his former girlfriend, paying for many things which should be shared equally between the two parents, as well as doing many things to be helpful and well liked. He loves his child and pretends not to be bothered when he is asked to do special favors for the mother. He is, in essence, being manipulated. He always does what is asked, as he knows that he has no legal rights to his child and she could withhold visiting privileges at a whim. The mother's goodwill has been very important to him.

Meanwhile, he hadn't developed any new relationship of his own. He felt no one would put up with such an awkward situation until recently, when he met a woman who was happy to spend her weekends together with him and his son. They live together now and always include the boy in everything they do. It took a while for George to relinquish the Servant archetype and begin to empower himself in his family situation. He took steps to ensure he had a permanent place in his son's life, and he had to stand up to the boy's mother and confront her manipulative behavior to regain his sense of lost power. As he has become more empowered he also developed a better relationship with both his new partner, his former girl-friend and his son. All his relationships became healthier, in fact, once he stood up for himself.

# *Functional Archetype: The Warrior*

## Recognizing The Warrior

As we embark on exploring the nature of the Warrior, let us leave behind ideas or attitudes which reflect the Servant archetype. By letting go of old and well-worn attitudes, we make the space for our archetypes to heal and be transformed. The Warrior archetype lets us all be the hero or heroine in our own lives. We take control, harness our willpower and live from a solidly empowered position in our work, relationships and in the world around us. The more we can give ourselves permission to feel good in the power of our own energy, the more personal power we accumulate in our lives.

The Warrior is the strongest of all the personal archetypes. It operates primarily on an instinctual level and affirmatively and positively reflects our levels of self-confidence, self-worth and personal power.

This archetype focuses our strength and our ability to assert our right to be the best person we know how to be. This means doing what gives us joy and allowing ourselves to fully express our talents and gifts and also to say "no" when necessary. Our ability to stand up for ourselves is associated with this archetype. It is from this archetype that we make our stand in life.

The Warrior is a highly intelligent and aware archetype. It is masculine in nature and engages with life in an active and energetic way. It is, of course, pertinent to both sexes, especially now that we are seeing the Warrior archetype flourishing in women as they gather courage and strength to live their lives free of restraint and constriction.

In order for the Warrior to fully develop itself the psyche creates challenges the Warrior must face. This external impetus usually takes the form of rejection or opposition. It forces the Warrior to fall back on its internal sense of its strength, ability and self worth. In this way the Warrior archetype will harness its strength and power. It sharpens its proverbial sword and develops its esteem, confidence and wisdom for growth and personal development.

### The Warrior on the side of good

The Warrior uses every situation to help it develop intentionality and direction. It sees life as something to be conquered through right or might. This singular vision is based on its illusion of duality. Things will appear either as good or bad and the Warrior will naturally stand on the side of good and will strive to eradicate evil. It ruthlessly pursues opposition which it perceives as being against it. It stands up for itself, believes in itself and is optimistic and enthusiastic about putting itself forward.

The polarity of good and bad gives the Warrior the impetus it needs to fight for itself. It will throw itself into causes which will enhance its power and confidence. It will also oppose anything which it perceives as standing in its way or limiting it.

The Warrior archetype thrives on strife and conflict. It pits itself against chaos and emptiness and is constantly striving to make sense out of life and give it meaning. It has courage, foresight and power, but it doesn't see or accept that the separation and opposition it experiences is its own projection. It isn't an archetype at peace with life.

### Spiritual limitations

The Warrior believes in the material world and its divisions of power and strength. Its spiritual awareness does not extend to the ultimate reality that we are all one and that there is no separation.

Because the Warrior archetype relates to the world from its instincts, centered in the Solar Plexus, it has an affinity to the nature of power in all things. It experiences power played out in relationships, working situations and in life, and understands the way that people act out their aggression, anger and jealousy to substitute for their real sense of personal power. Its psyche is geared towards developing confidence, self-esteem and personal power. It is important for it to have a strong and resilient ego, and to strive for success in all it does. It is able to make money, seek pleasure, find intimacy and survive without jeopardizing its self-worth or integrity in any way. Indeed, everything it does heightens its sense of worth.

Many people achieve this level of empowerment and many more seek it, but the spiritual limitation of the Warrior is that it believes that its success is the result of its own doing. It can be shortsighted and not link its ego with its spiritual awareness because it feels it is solely responsible for all that happens in its life. A spiritual Warrior, on the other hand, is constantly thankful for the challenges and obstacles it faces because it knows the way it grows and develops is by facing life with grace and grit. If the Warrior archetype does not develop a spiritual philosophy of life it remains limited and can become rigid and arrogant. Its vision of life can be egocentric and static, focused only on its ambitions and success.

The Warrior archetype gives us the opportunity to experience our control of the world around us. When we embody this archetype we use power to make things happen for ourselves and others. As well, we develop a capacity to achieve results and make things work; we gain a sense of mastery that we can survive crisis, stand alone in the face of conflict, recuperate from wounds and face uncertainty. It also represents our ability to stand up for ourself, feel worthy and express that worth in the form of confidence, healthy decisions and a joyful life. This is the spiritual Warrior's path.

The Warrior archetype offers us the opportunity to understand and come to terms with the nature of power. It gives us an awareness of how we manage power and how other people can harness it or misuse it in their lives and relationships. It is a necessary archetype to transcend on our path to love.

# DEVELOPING THE WARRIOR

## Taking Responsibility For Yourself

As you take responsibility for yourself it becomes necessary to call back the projections of power which you gave away to others. It is then that you can reinvest yourself with what you have given away.

Taking responsibility for your projections is necessary if you want to grow and develop your self worth. The degree of power you experience in your life is commensurate with your self-worth. As this becomes more developed you will meet challenges and opposition more easily and stop blaming or giving away power to others.

Giving away your power takes many forms. You can give power to others to heal you, help you or even hurt you. Owning your part in any situation helps you to take your power back.

## Exercise

**1** Think of three people (more if you like) whom you consider to be powerful. You can choose anyone—perhaps a politician, film actor or a parent.

**2** When you have these people in mind look carefully at them and define what it is that you consider to be powerful about them. For instance, you may say these people are powerful because they do exactly what they like or they have influence or are capable of saying "no" when they don't like or agree with something. They may also express themselves with a creativity and authority which you admire.

**3** Standing in front of a mirror say to yourself "I am …," listing the qualities you projected into your chosen people, such as "I am influential. I can say no. I can make things happen." Repeat this exercise several times until you feel that you have integrated the qualities you have projected into others.

This exercise is a good way to own your power. It helps you see how you give your power away to others and helps you to own your projections.

Whatever you admire or despise in someone else is always a part of yourself. You and I could each look at the same three people and see totally different things in them. No quality is a given truth. It is the reflection and projection of our own psyches which we are seeing all the time in everything we perceive as external reality. The skill of consciousness-raising is getting yourself to own your power by reclaiming what you have projected into others, into your relationships and the world around you.

## The Myth Of The Warrior Archetype

As we examine the myth of the Warrior archetype, ask yourself how you feel about power. Do you want power over others to tell them what to do or do you want personal empowerment which lets your own unique light shine in the world? Look at the myths around power which, along with love, are usually involved with every drama, fairy tale and characterization passed down through the ages. The theme of power and its abuse prevails still because we are only just learning to call on our own natural power for healing, health and wholeness.

The myth of the Warrior is based on the idea that we are separate and need to fight our way through life, imposing our will on others in order to gain the things we want. This myth lets us justify both control and dominance over others. It demands that those who embrace its ethos give over their hearts and consciousness to the path of power. There is little room for them to enjoy a peaceful spirit or a creative nature. The path of power is a myth developed in our Western culture as an ideal model which makes ruthlessness and bad behavior acceptable to many people. We may have success, money and power but unless we have love and peace of mind there is no real empowerment. The distinction between power and empowerment is that power exists in the external world, while empowerment is a function of being.

Be willing to look at your myths about power. Is it something you want or which you feel eludes you? And what will you do to achieve it?

Can you differentiate between empowerment and power? Power is empty without personal empowerment and this is something each person must develop in themselves.

## MEDITATION

Sit or lie in a comfortable position. Burn a candle or incense to cleanse the energy around you and take several deeply relaxing breaths as you begin to free your body from tension. Breathe into the tense places and feel relaxed as you begin to release tension.

Focus your awareness into your Solar Plexus. This is at the bottom of the sternum in the center of your rib-cage, just above your stomach. Visualize strong rays of light radiating from it. The rays shine outward and become stronger as you become more aware of your power. Continue your breathing in a relaxed and rhythmic way and let your awareness focus in your body. As you breathe be aware of releasing all constriction and tightness in your Solar Plexus.

Open yourself to the possibility of living from your strength in a positive and easy way. Be willing to let your light shine so that you can be the radiant person you know you are. Love yourself and let yourself be worthy of the love and respect you feel you deserve. Relax into yourself and feel power flowing through your body as you say YES to yourself and YES to your life.

## Vitality

As you open yourself to your power you will need to channel the energy flowing through your body. This means that you can use this energy for your creativity and health. You can focus it wherever you like. It can be used for your well-being and aliveness. Be sure it brings you joy. As you let your light shine for others remember to let it shine for yourself.

Begin to imagine that you are drawing energy in through your Solar Plexus. This energy takes the form of light and goes into every cell of your body. Its color is golden. Your eyes and skin become radiant and your muscle tone is smooth and youthful. Your bones and nerves are strong and resilient. Your hair shines and your eyes sparkle. Feel your vitality rise and your strength increase. You are empowering yourself right now with universal energy and the power of positive thought.

You may want to consider doing something which enhances your physical stamina and helps you build strength. You could try the following.

Walking

Jogging

Dancing

Swimming

Weight training

Yoga

Aikido

Judo

Alexander Technique

Massage

These activities help you to release tension and to focus your power.

## Empowerment

The way to empower yourself is to be certain of your self-worth. You are worth it! (Whatever it is you feel you want or deserve.) Say or write these affirmations with a sense of your entitlement.

*Divine power moves through me.*

*I value who I am.*

*I am worth my weight in gold.*

*I am worthy of my own self love.*

*I am the only person in my life who I am responsible for making happy.*

*I am free to choose love, joy and happiness in my life.*

*I am open to receiving love, happiness, health and prosperity, knowing that I deserve them all.*

*Goodness and joy are mine. I deserve them.*

*I own my power and I am willing to take responsibility for myself in all situations.*

*I am willing to grow and mature into the best person I can be.*

*I reclaim my power now.*

*I am the only person who knows what is best for me.*

*I stand up for myself and demand the very best for my efforts and abilities.*

## Case Histories

### *Janine*

Janine is a professional consultant who works with corporate management. She is a Warrior archetype and prides herself on her ability to "shake and move" people. She is very authoritative and even fearsome to people who don't know her well. She has described the work she does as helping people find their power. She has a highly developed ego and her lifestyle reflects it.

She maintains a high standard of living which includes expensive clothes, chic restaurants and luxury vacations. She is, however, not very happy, nor is she able to have intimate connections with people in her life. She came to see me because she was having a series of disturbing dreams over a period of several months. These dreams frightened her and gave her the impetus to look inward. As we worked together, it became evident that her life was missing spontaneity, joy and intimacy. She began to let go of her idea that she was superior to other people. Keeping herself separate was as much a defense as part of her strength. She developed this as a way of resisting opposition, but, in fact, she found herself very lonely.

As she transcended her Warrior archetype she dropped her defensive protection, and she became softer and more accessible to people around her. She enjoyed herself more and developed new friendships. As she lightened up, she was even able to laugh at her own haughtiness. As people got to know her better they were able to appreciate her strength and sense of fairness. She became a warmer and more loving person as she moved on from the Warrior archetype and felt less need to prove her worth. She found the path of the heart as she softened to let love into her life. What she has experienced in giving up separation is being able to live from her heart.

## Phillip

Phillip is a young man in his early thirties who came to see me for reasons unrelated to his personal life. He had a strong interest in psychic matters and wanted to know if I could help him. As we talked, I told him I was more involved with personal development work and felt that this was the key to many doors. He decided he wanted to work on himself and develop his inner being.

As Phillip's ego strength began unfolding, and he became more empowered and less self-effacing, something happened to him which made me feel that I was witness to the Warrior archetype emerging in his personality.

Phillip's employer was a strong Warrior archetype who had started his own business and made a success out of it. He chose young, ambitious people like Phillip to work for him. What he created was a group of young Warrior archetypes who eventually decided to challenge his authority and break away from him to form their own company.

This challenge to his authority came in the form of "We can do it better," a characteristic expression of the Warrior archetype. It is only through creating challenges like this that the Warrior archetype can develop and thrive.

The old employer was so angered at what happened that he challenged the group in a court battle in the hope of breaking their spirit. It was a fraught and tense time for Phillip. He would come to his sessions with me berating this man, and portraying him as vicious and ruthless. The irony was that as this fight went on, Phillip was developing the same qualities he accused his boss of having, only he was blind to this mirror in front of him. He wanted his own authority and challenging his boss was the way he hoped to get it. When he eventually recognized the opposition as his own projections, this situation began to ease up and his boss dropped the law suit. Phillip became clear about his desire for power and once he owned it for himself, was able to let go, and be more flexible and more gracious.

# 6

# THE HEART CHAKRA
Love, joy, unity, kinship and peace

DYSFUNCTIONAL ARCHETYPE:
*The Actor/Actress*

FUNCTIONAL ARCHETYPE:
*The Lover*

## HOW THE HEART CHAKRA FUNCTIONS

The Heart chakra functions as the core of our physical bodies and our spiritual essence. As the heart is the most important organ in our body, known as the Emperor in Chinese medicine, so love is the center of our lives. The Heart chakra allows us to imbue our physical life with the radiance of love, joy, unity, and kinship, and stimulates our sense of touch and delight in life. It is from the spiritual heart that the deepest meaning of life is felt and expressed.

To flourish and develop as a compassionate and loving person we need to be receptive to love. When our hearts are open we are at peace with ourselves and with those around us and we feel harmoniously balanced within ourselves. The experience of love helps us make fuller connections to the beauty and light of other people, as well as ourselves. Love is, after all, the foundation of life.

We are born with open Hearts, but as we enter into the illusions of life which separate us off from the eternal presence of love we shut our hearts down. In this world we need protection for our innocence, our purity and our joy. It is not safe to stay open and vulnerable to the harsh reality of other people's negativity and fear. We could not survive feeling totally exposed to others' pain. As we grow older we learn to protect this vulnerability by closing our Heart center down. Unfortunately we lose our capacity to trust in the ever-present goodness of life and find ourselves fixed in a groove of discontent and unhappiness. What we most long for and desire is then unavailable to us and we may find that we are starving for love. We may try many things to cover the feeling of emptiness, from drugs and sex, to overeating or overworking. We can pretend we are sophisticated and that love doesn't matter to us, but we know in our hearts that it is the only thing that truly counts in our lives and there is no substitute to cover its loss.

When we fall in love we are the most alive and joyful we can possibly be. We have found a significant other to share ourselves with and to know all the glory that God intended us to experience. When we are in love we are at one with ourselves and with all life.

The two archetypes which exemplify the energy of the Heart chakra are the Actor/Actress and the Lover. One is an archetypal portrait of the pretense of love which is not truly integrated in its experience. The other archetype is completely open to and enjoys the wonder of love.

## *Dysfunctional Archetype: The Actor/Actress*

◆

### Recognizing The Actor/Actress

The dysfunctional archetype of the Heart chakra, the Actor/Actress, refers to those who play at love but who are not sufficiently aware and hide their darker feelings under the hidden agendas of power and dominance. This archetype is incapable of real intimacy because it resists feeling its fears and negativity to loving and being loved by another. It goes through life acting as though everything were fine, escaping its inner emotional reality and managing to avoid the experience of intimacy. It never seems to get too close to anyone and avoids bonding by acting out its conflicts in tension and drama and distancing itself. It doesn't expose its own vulnerability and feels safe only at a distance from those it professes to love. Love, for this archetype, is a mental exercise rather than a function of its heart.

When anyone comes too close to its vulnerable core it closes down and sabotages its relationships. Its pain comes from old hurts and is expressed in holding back feelings or using arguments and a variety of other tactics to keep love away. Its neurosis, or fear of love, can become reactivated whenever someone penetrates too close to its old wounds. The threat is too great and leaves it terrified and afraid of losing its control. It is difficult to let go of the pain and let love into its life. In its attempt to defend itself from hurt it can do damage to those who mistake its charm for love and its willingness to bond with a fear of being alone. For the Actor/Actress can be very seductive and able to draw to it people who are able to give love, but it hides a closed and well-fortified heart.

There are many people who have achieved deep levels of love and happiness in their lives. You can see it on their faces and hear it in their voices. These are people who have made their peace with themselves and have opened their hearts to the gifts of love. They are able to accept others without criticism and they fully accept themselves, knowing that, at their core, they are love. The Actor/Actress maintains staunch defenses against the humbling and purifying experience of love. They desperately want it, and desperately need it, but at the same time are terrified of it. It would mean letting down all their defenses and being exposed.

The Actor/Actress harbors resentment about its past, often buried deep inside it for years, and this barrier keeps love away. It blocks its feelings and avoids opening to a richer and deeper understanding of itself because love is too painful. When it cuts off from love it diminishes its life force and dims its beauty. Opening its heart is not an act of will but, rather, a choice to include love in its life.

Being too vulnerable and protecting itself from hurt is the main concern of this archetype in an intimate relationship. It hopes to heal its wounds by finding someone to ease its pain and look after it, but it doesn't offer love in return. It finds it too hard to give from the heart. The push and pull aspect of its relationships is both frustrating and painful for anyone caught up in the tormenting games this archetype plays out.

### Beginning to change the Actor/Actress mentality

The Actor/Actress becomes enmeshed in co-dependent relationships which do not allow it to heal its wounds. It remains frozen in an emotional abyss and it is painful to witness this archetype struggling with its neurotic patterns of resisting love. If it remains unawares or keeps on blaming its partner, it will repeat the same old patterns over and over again. It needs to do what it longs for the most; that is to open its heart and love.

It takes a willing mind to realize we are projecting on to our partners in our attempt to resolved our wounds, but that is the way to free ourselves and let our hearts open to love. We can hope to find release from our pain by seeing our patterns and ending the struggle and conflict we have set up against being loved.

# MOVING ON FROM THE ACTOR/ACTRESS

## Taking Responsibility For Yourself

Taking responsibility for this archetype is a stage of development many people have to go through before finding real love. As adolescents we learn to imitate those who are in love; we learn how to behave in relationships.

Eventually we develop a capacity to love. This may come when we bond with another, feel safe and open our hearts in trust and faith. Sometimes, because of our fears, we remain blocked in a shallow facsimile of love, avoiding confrontation or difficulties which would enable us to deepen our relationships. We may find ourselves embroiled in fights and still not grasp the meaning of what love is for us. It is only when we drop our defenses and expose our soft, vulnerable nature that love has a chance to bloom and we can move on to the Lover archetype.

## Exercise

To help you deepen your capacity to love ask yourself the following questions.

1 Are you able to be open and honest about your feelings with another person?

2 How much love do you feel for yourself?

3 Can you experience love for yourself when you are unhappy or lonely?

4 Are you able to sustain a commitment through difficult times?

5 Do you know how to stay with someone through the unpleasant and hard times when communication is blocked because of blame or resentment?

**6** Can you be detached enough to allow your loved ones to be themselves?

**7** Does your love help you to honor your commitment to work things through when you feel unsure and vulnerable?

**8** Can you be true to your feelings in a relationship without sacrificing or losing your sense of self?

**9** Can you love someone as they are and not expect them to change for you?

**10** Can you love yourself enough to be the way you are in a relationship?

These questions are designed to give you some insight into your capacity to love and be loved. They are not a test with right or wrong answers, only a gauge for your understanding of love in your life.

## The Myth Of The Actor/Actress Archetype

As we move from the realm of the Actress/Actor archetype, we have the opportunity to examine our myths regarding love. It is important for our growth and development that we avoid mistaking need, dependency and gratitude for love. Love is the capacity to feel and express the deepest parts of ourselves with another.

Love is the building block of the universe and an essential component in our lives. Without love our lives are dry and stagnant. Love is the juice that keeps our energy flowing and bonds our spirits to our daily lives. It is up to us to choose to let it into our lives as well as give it to ourselves.

We could not exist without love. It is important to let go of any ideas we have about how love should be. It exists in so many ways and in so many forms that our imaginations could not fathom the bounty of love we experience at every moment. If we qualify love and insist that it must be a certain way we are not being loving, we are being controlling. The more we can expand our hearts to include others, without qualifying how they should be, the better we are able to let love flow into our hearts.

Be willing to look at your ideas about love and see if you can be gentle and kind to yourself as you release any limiting or narrow attitudes and myths which limit love in your life.

Relationships are the most difficult things in life to master. They require a willingness to open our hearts and let love purify us. Everyone is dealing with the whole of the collective unconscious and at least two entire family histories when we enter into a relationship. It takes a quiet perseverance and trust in love to open and be ourselves with someone. The love which flows through our hearts is the universe's gift to all who allow it in. See if you can risk being open to love.

# MEDITATION

Sit comfortably so that you are relaxed. Take a few deep breaths and let yourself settle into a meditative state where you feel at ease and comfortable. Let your body relax, let your emotions be tranquil and get a clear and strong sense of who you are as you go inside yourself. Release tension in your chest and focus your awareness in your heart. Repeat the words to yourself: I am love. I am love. Allow your chest to expand and fill with your breath as you do this. Be still in yourself as you repeat this phrase. Allow your gentle and tender nature to emerge as you allow love to flow in your heart. Be the most tender, loving person you can imagine being. Allow yourself to say: I love everything about myself. I am my own best friend in life and I trust in love.

Experience a flow of energy moving through your heart and down through your body as the love you feel expands to include people you know and care for. Keep expanding this love to include everything around you and eventually to include the whole planet. See the planet embraced in your arms and know that you are healing the world as you send love out from your heart. Gently relax and be at peace with yourself as you realize that you are the source of love in your life.

## Vitality

To vitalize your heart do those things which make you happy. It is important to know for yourself what gives you joy and happiness. It may be something very simple. Here are some ideas.

Play with a child or a pet

Look at a beautiful garden

Walk by the sea

Laugh at a funny film

Work on your car

Proceed with a creative project

Anything which makes you feel happy and joyful is good for your heart and will give you the energy you need for doing the things in your life that are less heartfelt. Being happy is important. Take some time to ask yourself what are the things and people that give you joy in your life and watch your vitality pick up.

## Empowerment

When we make the choice to open our hearts we are empowering our lives in the most essential way because we are making a choice for love and happiness. Being receptive to love is how we choose to let love into our lives. We are enhanced in every way when we choose to do this. Saying the following affirmation helps you to open your heart to love.

*Love is my reason for being.*

*I allow love to come into my life and fill me with happiness and joy.*

*Love is who I am.*

*Love is for all.*

*I open my heart and rejoice in my being.*

*I open my heart and accept others as they are.*

*I release my pain and forgive the past. I am free to love.*

*I am in tune with the love that fills the universe.*

*I am at one with all life.*

*Love fills my heart with joy.*

*Love is the best thing for me.*

*I share my love with all who accept it.*

*I accept the love of all who give it.*

## Case Histories

### *Harriet*

Harriet is a woman in her late forties with three children. She has been divorced for many years. She was chronically depressed and had not had a meaningful or enduring relationship for some time. She'd had affairs with married men or those who lived far away. She had sex with many men, but always avoided real intimacy. This was also true in her relationships with women. As soon as anyone became too friendly with her she would sabotage the friendship in some way or for some reason.

Her friends tended to be people who could help her and look after her when she got depressed. She attracted rescuers who would eventually become exasperated with her for not taking responsibility for herself. They would eventually leave her; and thus create an even deeper sense of rejection. She was lonely and also very jealous of other people's happiness.

Her heart remained closed through years of therapy and workshops. Though she could cry for her pain, she still denied love in her life. She felt she deserved love, but she did not know how to give it. Her immature and inappropriate defense patterns had been carried over from her early childhood when her father abandoned the family and she was left to help her grieving mother. As an adult, she needed to choose to let love into her life, even though it meant confronting her pain from the past and releasing it.

It became clear to her, after years of pretending, that her life was not fine the way it was. She needed to make changes in her attitudes and look within herself. She was going to have to choose love and find her happiness in giving to others with an open heart.

She enrolled on a healing course which gave her the opportunity to have meaningful contact with people. She struggled with a jealous and vindictive nature, but gradually became conscious of her old patterns and stopped pushing others away. She created more opportunities for friendship in her life and let herself experience how desperately she longed for love. Slowly her heart melted and she began to let love in. Intimacy no longer terrified her, and she was able to form deep friendships with both men and women. She was fortunate that she chose to let love into her life. She was so desperate for it that she was on the brink of suicide. It took being pushed to her knees before she opened her heart. When she did release her pain, she received everything she had hoped for in her life.

## Thomas

Thomas is a man in his early fifties who spent his life in pursuit of learning. He wanted knowledge so that he could become a great spiritual teacher. He spent many years studying Eastern and Western healing techniques, and was a member of several spiritual organizations. He was divorced and had an endless stream of women friends, but no enduring intimate relationships. He was always more interested in developing his reputation and his work as a healer than in pursuing a healthy and intimate relationship.

In truth, his heart was closed. He never let anyone close to him for fear they would see his vulnerability and exploit him. Yet, in his work as a healer he demanded that his clients expose their pain to him. His voyeuristic nature was exploitative and manipulative of the people he treated.

His life was filled with an endless variety of activity which involved other people, but no one could get too close to him for very long. Very few people tried to penetrate his defenses because he was skillful at using his knowledge as a weapon and keeping them away. He was very well armed with knowledge, but deficient in his capacity to love.

It took several very painful situations to bring him to a place where he needed to ask others for help, but when the crisis passed he still had not opened his heart. He struggled with his pride and was often very lonely. He has, however, remained fixed in this archetype, unwilling or unable to make the shifts that he needs in order to find healing. Hopefully one day he will feel safe enough to open his heart. This choice has to be his. Loving is not dependent on the amount of knowledge we have, but rather on our ability to recognize in another that same need which we have in ourselves. This is everyone's realization about love. From this place we take the risk to be vulnerable, expose our pain and trust that we are worthy of love just as we are.

## *Functional Archetype: The Lover*

### Recognizing The Lover

Opening to the Lover archetype within ourselves means we first and foremost love ourselves. Without knowing who we are and understanding and accepting ourselves, we cannot fathom the power of love. Leaving behind the Actress/Actor archetype creates the opportunity for change and healing to happen. Our hearts are open, waiting for the spark of love to ignite the passions we have for life. As this flame burns, it clears away the dross of incomplete and unfulfilled experiences which created pain and forced us to shut down. As we choose love we also choose life. As we affirm ourselves, love eases its way into every fiber of our being.

The Lover archetype lives its life from a place of love. This is an archetype which loves people, animals, plants and all of life. It especially loves and accepts itself as whole and complete, and knows how absolutely worthy it is to receive love.

The Lover archetype is neither exclusive nor limited in its capacity to love. It is open to anyone who comes within its sphere and expresses respect and warmth. We know when we are in the presence of the Lover archetype with its open heart, because we feel well in ourselves, happy to be who we are and not judged. To the Lover we are enough, perfect as we are. When love moves through the open heart of the Lover it embraces everyone and everything in its radiant energy field. Can you remember falling in love and feeling everything in the world was beautiful? This is the energy of the Lover. The glowing energy of this archetype expands and fills our whole being with love and joy. It makes the world a richer and happier place in which to be. We are drawn to the Lover because its energy feeds our deepest sense that we too can be this open and expansive when we open ourselves to love.

The Lover has chosen to open its heart to life. It has an on-going love affair with all things and no matter how many obstacles are put in its way it will always choose love and life. It accepts negativity and challenge as part of life's program for growth and maturity. Its joy melts hardened and resistant attitudes.

This archetype is suited to those people who are free of spirit and generous by nature and who are happy with life. Its joy is not dependent on circumstances, places or conditions. Its inner glow emanates from the center out and is all-embracing.

The Lover draws people to it wherever it goes and is often cherished by children and old people. They sense the Lover's abundant energy and are instantly attracted to it. The whole world loves a lover and this archetype is able to love with real gusto. The Lover is always affirmative and positive, giving itself fully to any situation or project in which it is involved. It has a great capacity to laugh and find joy in the lighter side of life. It has an ability to create joy where there was little before.

The Lover is a wonderful archetype. It is depicted in the Tarot as the Fool who marches through life ready to step over the cliff into the abyss, seemingly oblivious to any peril. The Lover survives difficult times because it knows that life itself is a joy and little else matters without love. The Lover is in touch with its feelings and has a profound sense of the moment. It loves to share its good feelings. It seems to miss the heaviness and despair of those people with highly developed intellects who suffer from the pain they see around them. The Lover delights people with its ability to make a difficult situation seem easy and people long to be near it because it is a tonic to their soul.

# DEVELOPING THE LOVER

## Taking Responsibility For Yourself

Taking responsibility for the love in our lives is a major part of our development. This means we are able to forgive when we've been hurt and let go of the past, releasing our feelings and living in the present, the only place where love can be experienced. Taking responsibility for this archetype means living actively in the now and loving everything that goes on in life just as it is; the pain, the grief, the anger and the frustration, as well as the fun, happiness, love and serenity; the entire spectrum of life is ours to cherish and love. All the things we feel that grind us down can be transformed when we love our life just the way it is. Love is an active, present-based experience which is not exclusive and includes the dirty and ugly as well as the majestic and beautiful.

Love it all, the gurus tell us, be with it and be one with it. Learning to love it as it is is part of our awakening, and as we experience this we make our lives a unique expression of the love within us.

## Exercise

If you find dealing with the feelings that you experience in this exercise too difficult to handle, don't attempt it until you feel ready to work through what you have resisted.

1 Forgiving and releasing the past takes courage. Are you willing to forgive those who hurt you and release the pain of separation, hurt and loss? Forgiving usually starts with forgiving our parents. They are the core relationship from which we form our character and from which we create the delusions which separate us from love. Look carefully at your parents or primary caretakers and be willing to forgive them for their limitations to loving you. Release your feelings about not feeling that you had enough of what you wanted or deserved. Try to realize that they were doing the best they could with their own limitations. This may help you to forgive them more easily. You can start with a simple sentence like: "I forgive you and let go of the past."

**2** Now move on to forgive anyone you feel didn't love you in the way you wanted to be loved. This can include former friends, lovers, partners, colleagues, teachers and so on. These can be people from your past or from the present. Again, saying a simple sentence like the above will do.

Repeat the sentence and consciously try to let go of your resentment.

Your Higher Self, which is so closely linked to your heart, will protect you from being overwhelmed by negative feelings that you are unable to handle. Trust yourself to find the love in your heart that you need for this exercise.

**3** Forgive yourself for being hard on yourself, for your self-criticism and self-punishment. You may have felt it was your fault for not receiving the love you needed in the past. Love yourself now and be willing to make yourself right for your needs, desires and feelings. Be responsible for the love you want in your life.

Acknowledge that it is your right to be loved and to give love fully.

Loving yourself is the most important thing you can do for yourself at this moment. Accept yourself and the situation you find yourself in. This acceptance will heal your heart and let love flow into your life.

## The Myth Of The Lover Archetype

As we accept the Lover archetype and deepen and enrich our sense of self, it is important to believe in and acknowledge our own *rightness*. This means that the feelings we have are all right, as are the things we do, the way we think and even the way we behave. They all reflect the love or lack of love that we experience.

When we collude with the dark, negative side of people or situations, we are saying there isn't enough love in our lives or that we are not capable of generating the quantity of love sufficient to heal a situation or person. If it is not within us, then where is it? Whom do we need to call to get it?

It is within every one of us to be able to love, heal and transform the pain, loss and separation in this world. We start with ourselves and extend this love to every situation and person we encounter. This is how love heals the world.

Many people feel there isn't enough love in their lives. As we develop we learn that love is literally all around us and we have access to the love which resides deep within us. We can choose to be at one with this love whenever we open our hearts. When we have conflicts or difficult times it is all too easy to blame others or ourselves for how it is. At times like this we need to remember to continue to love and value ourselves. Invariably we find these times put us in touch with our own soft and gentle feelings and this expands our awareness and let us accept ourselves and others with love. When we connect to the deep center of being, which is the heart, and live from this place as consistently as we can, our wounds can mend from the damage of our past. We never heal the heart when we are cruel, angry or trying to get even for the hurt done to us. In order to feel the joy that lives within we need to let go and let our inner light shine on the world around us, accepting, forgiving and knowing that what is truly sacred is the love we share with others.

Love is not conditional on what we have, what we do, where we live. It is God's gift to us as part of his love for us and when we learn that we are love itself we are more capable of living in the light of our own heart. The path of the heart is simple and truthful.

If you feel you are unable to experience love then it is important to look at the attitudes which are standing in your way. Did someone tell you, consciously or unconsciously, that you weren't good enough for love? And did you believe this and take this on as part of your emotional reality? So many people believe they are not lovable. Part of the narcissism of our culture is that we truly believe we are not enough as we are and that we must prove we are good enough before we receive the love we so rightfully deserve. Resentment blocks our capacity to feel the love which is present for us.

The more we can openly acknowledge the pain of our past hurts and release the grief we carry we free ourselves to live in the light of the moment. Love exists in the now and experiencing this is the purpose of being here. Releasing the past, living in the present and experiencing ourselves as the source of love and joy is what spiritual growth is about.

# MEDITATION

Sit in a comfortable position where you can be relaxed. Take several deep breaths and release any tension you feel in your body. Bring your awareness up into your Heart chakra. Feel the quality of energy which surrounds your heart. Is it heavy and leaden? Is it tight and congested? Is it light or soft?

As you sit and breathe gently say to yourself: "I open my heart to love. I choose love." Feel your heart expand as love moves through your body. Trust that your experience of this energy is real. The more you trust in love the more it becomes a part of your life.

## Vitality

Some activities seriously damage a sensitive heart. For instance, smoking and heavy drinking weaken the heart, both physically causing damage and psychically blocking energy coming into the Heart chakra.

Excessive activity of any kind, even fun, can also be hard on the heart. This is the center of balance and asks a balanced and healthy lifestyle to help it work on your behalf. The heart asks that we love ourselves in every activity we do.

Are you doing anything to excess? Are you working too much? Drinking too heavily? Do you smoke or eat too much? Are you getting enough rest, play and affection? Everything you do for yourself which makes you happy keeps your heart healthy and make love easier to give and receive.

If you can change your lifestyle to give your heart a chance to work for you without too much stress and strain then you are doing something to love yourself. Your heart will always support you by giving you the vitality you need for your life's activities. It is not just physical muscles which pump your life's blood, but an emotional receptor for the love in our lives as well.

A list of activities which are good for the heart include the following.

Seeing or phoning someone you love and enjoy being with or talking to

Writing a letter to someone you miss

Taking photos of people and things you love and putting them somewhere you can draw on that love whenever you look at them

Having a party for someone you love to honor them on their birthday or celebrate an achievement

Giving yourself flowers

Smiling at yourself every time you catch your eye in the mirror

Watching a good romantic film or reading a wonderful love story

Wearing pink—the color of love

## Empowerment

The affirmations which help you to open your heart are designed to encourage you to feel comfortable with love. It is important to build your trust in love and that requires being affirmative and positive. The more you can be yourself and open your heart the more easily love can flow in your life.

Say the following affirmations to yourself in a gentle and loving way. They can be said standing in front of a mirror so you can see the love in your eyes and can open your heart to yourself.

*I love and accept myself just as I am.*

*I am perfectly myself and love the me I know myself to be.*

*I forgive the past in love and release pain, doubt and fear.*

*I am one with the universal force within. I am one with love.*

*Love is my reason for living.*

*I love freely and unconditionally.*

*Love opens me to new realms of being.*

*Love is the center of my life.*

*I choose to love.*

*I trust in love.*

*I give myself the largest share of my own love.*

*Love moves through me and connects me with the source of life.*

*Love heals me and sets my spirit free.*

## Case Histories

### Charlie

Many years ago I met a fellow searcher named Charlie who embodied the essence of the Lover archetype to me. He was highly intelligent and had studied physics at university before he left for a period of time to work in Antarctica. He came back a very conscious man, and became involved with esoteric healing and spirituality. I met him in a workshop called an "Enlightenment Intensive" in London. Sitting across from me, holding the question "Tell me who you are," as a meditation exercise, he began to radiate such an intensely powerful energy that people around him began to either cry or laugh. His Heart chakra was wide open.

This man was having a direct experience of himself as the source of love. His awareness of that touched everyone to their core that afternoon. Each of us experienced an opening of our own hearts as a result of being in his energy field. He had directly touched our spirits with his and I feel sure that wherever he is now, he is creating this same intense feeling of love around him. He was a rare and wonderful person to know.

### Gabrielle Roth

I met Gabrielle Roth in America. She was teaching dance workshops at Esalen Institute in Big Sur, California and, after being introduced to her and feeling the warmth and love radiating from her, I knew that I wanted

Heart chakra and our thoughts focused in the Brow chakra. When this bridge is flooded with energy, which is unexpressed emotion, it either stagnates and blocks the throat or, in a more healthy outlet, it gets channeled into creative expression. When there is no outlet to express feelings some form of expression must be found to vent unexpressed emotions.

The archetypes for this chakra naturally focus on the quality and intensity of our communication, or our lack of it. These archetypes are the Silent Child, who hides its true self away and is silenced by shame and hurt, and the Communicator, the adult who takes responsibility for its life and speaks up for what it wants and needs with clarity, direction and integrity.

## Dysfunctional Archetype: The Silent Child

### Recognizing The Silent Child

The Silent Child is an archetype describing levels of suppression where feelings of frustration, anger and sometimes violence have not been expressed. This archetype holds on to its feelings and does not reveal its hurt, pain or anger openly. Sometimes this energy is channeled into artistic or creative pursuits. At other times it simply sits and stagnates, producing a limited and depressed personality. This archetype stays closed in order not to reveal its intense pain and sorrow, or its abuse.

The Silent Child in its abuse or wounding hides its pain and shame. Its feelings get safely locked away and are not openly aired. It learns to feel safe in silence or jokingly hiding its true feelings. The Silent Child archetype can dampen its feelings with drugs, tobacco, alcohol and food. It will suppress what is too frightening or painful to express. Unfortunately, in order not to feel its grief or despair, this archetype will not express its creativity. Its life-force becomes weakened.

Substance abuse numbs and mutes the spirit which is why the Silent Child is attracted to it. It doesn't want to have to experience or express the pain it is holding on to. It has made a contract with itself to remain closed and not reveal its pain at any cost, even at the expense of its wellbeing and pleasure. It may channel this pain into creative action but it will not expose its true vulnerability for fear of recrimination or rejection.

The Throat chakra is naturally very delicate and when the Silent Child suppresses its vivacity and life force it makes this center—and all the others as well—contract, imploding energy which is meant to be expressed. The throat gets closed off when the Silent Child swallows words and feelings.

The Silent Child resists opening to what it perceives to be a threatening situation. It has been silenced for expressing itself and is familiar with difficult or even threatening situations. The Silent Child has been deeply affected by what was expressed to it and it has chosen to close off rather than share what it feels. This archetype will have to struggle to make itself heard and to feel that what it says counts. The life force may find non-verbal ways of expressing itself as well, for example in dance, dramatics or music.

The Silent Child is sensitive and feels the pain of separation acutely. It holds back its fears and tears, believing that expressing what it feels will lead to it being rejected or punished. It will lie to cover up and protect itself. This is damaging to one's natural integrity and limits the free flow of creative energy as well as the innate awareness that speaking up for one's self is essential to having what one wants in life.

### Beginning to change the Silent Child mentality

The Silent Child feels that what it wants or cares about is not important to those around it. It will struggle throughout its development to be able to express its needs and ask for what it wants without the fear of punishment or reprisal. It may take years of work and patient and gentle awareness before the Silent Child will speak up for itself. There can be grief and rage for needs which were never met and a pervading feeling of frustration when the awareness that it was never heard sinks into its consciousness. Yet it is in mourning this loss of self that the Silent Child learns to speak up for itself and to be heard. It may have such a constricted throat that actual words may not express the feelings which have been held back. When the feelings start to come they may be released as grunts and groans, shouts and infantile tantrums. They reflect the original pain of not being seen, loved or heard.

The Silent Child may go through life projecting on to the world that no one loves or listens to them. If this is so, it must own its projection in order to heal its wounds and change its reality.

If there has been emotional suppression in the past the throat becomes the focal point for the unexpressed fears, tears and anger which were not said. The neck muscles will become rigid and feel like strong cords of tension. There can also be chronic sore throats, problems with the mouth and jaw and hearing difficulties when the emotions are blocked. The jaw tightens and the mouth and lips lose their sensuality; they become tight. No other center shows so vividly or so quickly the emotions we feel and need to express. The Silent Child has been prevented from speaking its truth at some point in its development and has had to swallow its joy as well as its guilt and sorrow. This becomes a recurring pattern in later life if not recognized and changed. This archetype may even believe it is incapable of knowing what is true for it because of the degree of suppression it has imposed on itself in order to survive. It does not feel safe expressing its feelings and may not even know why this is so if the abuse or neglect happened in early childhood. It experiences its environment as far too hostile and unfriendly to ask for help or even to express its need for contact.

The Throat chakra relates to creativity and personal expression, and it is through creativity that the Silent Child transmutes its negative emotions into positive, life-affirming energy. Creative expression is what opens the doors for the Silent Child to come out of its dark cavern of pain and enter the world of light and kinship.

Many creative people have experienced childhood trauma and live out the Silent Child archetype. They act, sing or perform to express the vital energy they have suppressed. Everyone needs the space to express their thoughts, dreams and hopes in a meaningful way. This is part of our freedom and a signpost of our individuality. Self pity is often the result of not being listened to or being believed. The Silent Child needs to express its inner reality and communicate its sensitivity to find a positive release for itself. This is how to transform the pain.

## MOVING ON FROM THE SILENT CHILD

### Taking Responsibility For Yourself

Taking responsibility for our thoughts and feelings may be easy but saying what we feel and expressing our needs to others can feel like the most threatening thing on earth. When we are faced with exposing our vulnerability, feeling the degree of our damage and pain, or taking the risk of looking foolish and being rejected, we keep our thoughts and feelings to ourselves. Overcoming our timidity and shyness seems like a formidable task and expressing our real self takes courage. It takes a strong sense of self acceptance to realize that what we have to say is important and valuable.

If we want to heal we need to be willing to express our feelings and speak the truth about our pain. We can do this with a friend, a partner or a therapist, someone who is on our side and who values us for our efforts at being whole and complete. Keeping our feelings hidden doesn't serve our physical or emotional health and it makes others responsible for knowing what we want and need. As adults who communicate we are able to take the load off others to know what we want and need. If someone is really able to be there for us in our emotional turmoil we are blessed. If we are alone with the pain we can ask for help from a minister, a priest or anyone who is professionally capable of supporting others through crisis. Holding our pain inside does not serve our well-being or growth. Learning how to communicate is essential for our development.

## Exercise

1  Reflect on a situation in your life when you wanted to say something and were unable to express yourself. Remember what you were feeling at the time. Were you feeling that if you spoke up you would be laughed at or ignored? Were you afraid of not being recognized or of not being listened to? Did you remain quiet but harbor resentment?

2  Visualize this situation again and allow yourself to express what you would have liked to say at the time. You may realize that your thoughts and ideas were valuable and that you had something important to contribute. Realizing this may evoke feelings of sadness or anger at not having been listened to. Allow these feelings to come to the surface and give yourself the opportunity to experience them. Let go of any feelings of humiliation or fear which you associate with them.

3  Now say to yourself: "People listen to me and value who I am." Repeat this over and over to yourself as you integrate the truth of this into your awareness. You may wish to consider the possibility that if some people can't hear what you have to say it may be that they are not ready to hear what you have to tell them. Perhaps you may want to be with people who do want to know what you are able to share with them. As you open yourself to new possibilities for your self expression be aware that your contribution is important to others as well as yourself.

**4** Consider keeping a journal in which you write down your feelings and ideas. You may be surprised at how astute your thoughts and perceptions are about yourself or others. You will also have the opportunity to see the misconceptions and negative attitudes which are blocking your happiness. This is your way of giving yourself a voice and having the space to be heard.

## The Myth Of The Silent Child Archetype

Our voices can hardly be heard over the din of traffic, television and piped music that is all around. It is as though there is a conspiracy to drown out the voice of the individual. Many well-known people in high places have also been caught lying. There seems to be little validation for tranquillity or for speaking the truth.

Many people become uncomfortable with their feelings and shy away from expressing them when there is space in which to open up. And yet without expressing our personal truths, saying what is real for us and living from the depth of our integrity we have little chance of developing into whole and balanced individuals capable of sustaining deep and intimate relationships.

Look at the myths of the Silent Child and be willing to let go of your suppressed feelings. Perhaps as a child you were told to be quiet and be good. You associate silence with compliance and speaking out with rebellion. Certainly for many of us this was true. For many it was permissible to be happy but not to express sadness or unhappiness at home. It is important to know the level of personal expression you were allowed as a child because at some level your unwillingness or inability to speak up for yourself then will persist into your present experiences.

Did your parents encourage you to speak the truth or express yourself as a child? If you were not allowed personal expression you may find it frustrating and difficult to say how you feel now. You may believe that people don't care for what you have to say or that your contribution isn't important. You need to feel comfortable with expressing your truth.

Are you willing to give your thoughts and feelings room to be expressed? What about writing a poem, telling a story or finding another creative form which lets you express your imagination and inner reality?

Give yourself the pleasure of opening yourself to the beauty of self expression in whatever form appeals to you. It helps strengthen your being in every way.

## MEDITATION

Sit in a quiet place where you can relax. Allow your breathing to become slow and easy. Release any stress you feel in your body. Bring your attention to your throat, tongue, the inside of your mouth and the back of your neck. If you find any tension in these areas release it by breathing into them. Allow your breath to open your throat, relax your tongue and soften your hard palate. Imagine that the area of your hard palate is widening across your face and that your jaw is relaxing. Let your vocal chords relax and let your breath pass down deep into your lower back, expanding your waist as you inhale.

Visualize the back of your neck relaxing and opening as a beautiful blue light enters the back of your neck. This is the light of truth and it helps you to tap into your own truth. It enters the Throat chakra to help ease your fears about expressing yourself. Visualize this light becoming more intense as you breathe into your throat.

This will help you to speak up for yourself. It energizes your Throat chakra and stimulates your will-power, your creativity and your ability to communicate. As a consequence of expressing yourself you are able to enjoy good health, happiness and well-being. By saying what you want and need you ease your inner tension. You now have the ability to say what you wish and to trust you will be heard and your feelings acknowledged. Everyone enjoys what you have to say. Allow yourself to say out loud "I want … (fill in the blanks). I need … Please help me." As you sit silently listen to the words and respect whatever it is that you desire.

## Vitality

There are many good ways to energize your Throat center. Singing is the best and most fun way. Singing is putting words to the joy in your heart. You could also practice the whispered "ahs" used in the Alexander Technique. This is done by placing the tip of the tongue against the lower back teeth with the lips slightly parted. Breathe in through the nose and release your lower jaw to make the sound of "ah." Keep the jaw loose and relaxed. Practice this five times in a row. It helps to release the tension in the pelvis and lower back as well as the throat. There is a very strong connection between the two centers and by releasing the throat you energize the pelvis. Here are some other suggestions for energizing the Throat.

Chanting

Learning the drums

Keeping a journal in which you can safely record your thoughts and perceptions

Painting your self portrait

Listening to nature—to the dawn chorus, to the wind and rain

Saying no to people when they ask you to do something you don't want to do

Shouting your anger somewhere where you won't be overheard

## Empowerment

The best way to empower yourself is to speak your truth in the clearest way that you can. This means to "walk your talk" as the native Americans say. Having the integrity to say what you mean and mean what you say is what gives you credibility. The following affirmations can be said out loud to help you empower your self and find your voice.

*What I have to say is valuable to others.*

*I delight in expressing myself and I appreciate being listened to.*

*By expressing my truth others find the way to their truth.*

*Creativity is my birthright.*

*The truth sets me free.*

*I open myself to my truth. I listen to and honor myself.*

*I speak from my heart.*

*I honor my inner voice.*

*My voice resonates with my depth, beauty and truth.*

*I delight in sharing my truth with others.*

*I harness my will-power to serve my greatest good and highest joy.*

*Expression reflects my individual nature.*

*I am a joyful and creative soul.*

*I express the beauty and love of myself in everything I do.*

## Case Histories

### Marie

Marie is a young woman in her mid-thirties. She married young and raised her son on her own after divorcing his father. She worked as a cleaner in a hair salon, and suffered with chronic asthma and was plagued with migraine headaches. She smoked and drank heavily, especially on weekends and holidays. In the evening, when she was lonely, she played sad music and drank a bottle or more of wine. She felt her life was over at 37 and had no hopes or dreams for her future. All her longings were transferred into hopes for her son. She occasionally indulged in cannabis and other recreational drugs, and generally felt far worse for using them. She disliked her job and felt miserable about her life most of the time.

Because of her tendency for substance abuse, her willpower was weakened and it was difficult for her to find her way forward in life. Anything which required a sustained act of will was too much effort for her. Whenever she resolved to change her life, she would fall back into her old habits. This cycle undermined all her efforts to help herself.

When I met her for treatment, she spoke a bit about her childhood and how she was never allowed to express herself. Neither her family nor her husband had given her feelings any importance. She felt sure she would never achieve anything in her life. I suggested she try homeopathic treatment for her mental and physical symptoms. After a few treatments, when she had an acute flare-up of her throat problems, she stopped smoking and drinking. This made her start to think about how she had abused her body in the past.

As she started to feel better in herself, she was able to find a job in a local business. The work grew and she was given new responsibilities. She proved to be both bright and worth her weight in gold to her employers, who needed a trustworthy and responsible assistant. She gave up her cleaning job and retrained to develop skills which would help her go further in her new career. She stopped drinking, cut out drugs and developed stronger willpower. One of the benefits of her transformation was that she stopped having sore throats and headaches. She is now full of vitality and looking after her health. Her voice is deeper and richer. She looks like a new person and she feels she has a right to speak up for what she wants for herself.

## John

John is a teacher in a large educational institution. He experienced constant difficulties defining his job status in a department rife with intrigue and dissension. He never knew where he stood, or even if he would have his job from one term to the next. He tried to placate his bosses by working overtime for no extra pay, seeing students late in the evening and trying to show everyone what a likeable person he was. Hard as he tried, he couldn't communicate his needs to the people whom he worked under. They either failed to listen to him or blatantly ignored him.

He was desperate for recognition and to be heard. This, in fact, was a re-enactment of old family patterns where no one paid him attention or listened to his needs. He came from a large family where his parents were busy trying to make ends meet. They didn't have time for their own emotional needs, let alone those of their son.

As we all tend to do, he re-created a life situation which would help him heal his childhood wounds. He knew that it was important he be heard and he worked to develop his voice. On an inner plane he started meditating and listening to what his intuition told him. He began defining and expressing his boundaries clearly and stopped taking on work for which he was not paid. He started to value his talent, which had been seriously taken for granted by his bosses. Eventually they did acknowledge him, and started appreciating his consistency and willingness to make their department work. It coincided with his inner awareness of his own value.

Eventually, his personal expression and his self worth became stronger. Telling the truth about his feelings and recognizing his needs became a priority in his life. He found that problems cleared up faster and didn't fester when he spoke the truth about how he felt. He was more deeply in touch with his creativity as a result and began a writing course which eventually led to the publication of his first novel. He developed both his inner voice and his outer voice.

## *Functional Archetype: The Communicator*

### Recognizing The Communicator

Releasing the Silent Child archetype frees us to become clear and effective communicators. As the fear and doubts dissolve and we take responsibility for expressing how we feel and what we want in life, doors begin to open for us. Somehow actually saying how it is for us dissipates negative energy and lets more of what is good come our way.

The Communicator is the quintessential archetype of our time. It relates to anyone whose job or personal well-being is dependent on clear and direct communication. This also includes people involved in non-verbal communication such as art, music and dance. In an age where technology has provided us with several options for improving the quality of our communication this archetype is essential to integrate into our lives.

Technology has enabled us to have direct communication anywhere in the world within seconds. We are responsible for delivering quality communication which is direct, focused and clear. This is communication based on intent and delivered, hopefully, with integrity. The Communicator is an archetype for people who take responsibility for what they say and how they say it. Words have weight, and both professionally and personally the Communicator stands for what it says. It has a proper regard for the content of its message and a sense of respect for those with whom it is in contact.

Speaking up and being heard is an essential component of this archetype. The Communicator speaks from its Higher Self and expresses its feelings and thoughts with alacrity and purpose. It neither gossips, criticizes nor curses and has a special regard for the gravity of the spoken and written message. For those who embody this archetype their communication is enhanced by the connection between the deep core of the self, the inner workings of the heart and the exercise of the mind which are all linked by a clear intention to relate. This archetype knows that its spirit is diminished every time it lies, cheats or is grandiose. Even saying the words "I love you," which are so important to our well-being, can wound and hurt if they are not said sincerely. So the Communicator is careful not to wound or hurt with what it says and is mindful that its words are taken in and experienced by those being spoken to.

When this archetype says it is your friend you can bank on the trust that implies. When it says it will do something, it does so to the best of its ability. This willingness to keep its agreements and to foster trust and well-being is the strongest characteristic of this archetype. It does not let people down with empty promises or false hopes. It is sincere and backs up its words with right action. There is a strong sense of congruency between what it says and what it does.

This archetype represents anybody who delivers their words honestly and means what they say. This archetype stands by its word, can be trusted with vital information and can be relied upon to stand firm in the face of opposition to be true to itself and anyone it is connected with.

Many people today know the right words to say, especially in the psycholinguistics of the New Age or the business parlance of the market place, but few have either the life experience or the personal integrity to be able to stand for what they say as well. So the Communicator is an archetype that has sterling virtue in a world where the *sleaze factor* runs high and where words are cheap.

The Communicator is a positive model for our age. It is an archetype which overcomes all levels of negativity through being direct and positive. The Communicator lends energy and vitality to its communication, and there is a high degree of intention focused in what it says. The Communicator knows the importance of the spoken word and the healing power that comes from it.

The Communicator speaks both its mind and its heart. When it is angry it expresses it and when it is feeling gentle and open it is not afraid to show that as well. It also encourages others to speak their truths. Implicit in its actions is a strong sense of trust, reliability and groundedness which offers confidence and freedom of choice. Its words are not mesmerizing or hypnotic. There is no need to either manipulate or coerce. The Communicator understands that only the best things are created from free choice, and gives others the freedom and space to make their choices.

This archetype knows that clear communication helps people feel well in themselves and that being understood lets people know they are valued. It knows that true intimacy can only come when there is trust and it knows that when it expresses how it feels, others have the opportunity to respond from their feelings as well.

The intentions of the Communicator are as clear as its integrity. Open and direct communication frees it from complications and helps it to stay connected to its deep core.

# DEVELOPING THE COMMUNICATOR

## Taking Responsibility For Yourself

The Communicator is committed to both congruency and integrity in its actions and words. What this means is that the Communicator does what it says it will do. Its words reflect both integrity and its highest intention.

Everyone knows that words have power. They can hurt us or heal us. When we learn to allow our words to reflect our wisdom and our inner core than we will have achieved a very high level of development. Taking responsibility for what we say and how we say it is important. We don't need to be clever as much as honest, or amusing as much as clear in our communication. Words help us to connect our minds to our hearts. Words can heal us. When we take responsibility for what we feel and express what we want to say our words ring true. When we function as responsible communicators we bridge the gap between our mind and our feelings. We open the doors to being touched by the spirit of love embodied within every person's deep center. Communication, when it is conscious, can help us to find our way back to ourselves.

## Exercise

This exercise is useful in opening up the Throat chakra and allowing the Communicator archetype to evolve. It uses the words and expressions most people either resist saying or hearing.

1 Look in the mirror and say out loud to yourself: "You are beautiful/handsome and I love you." Allow your feelings to come to the surface as you look in your eyes. Let your words heal your pain and soothe away any sadness. Keep telling yourself these words until you feel your fears and loneliness start to melt away.

2 In your mind's eye visualize someone who has hurt you in the past. See if you can permit yourself to say those healing words to that person. Watch their pain begin to melt away their defenses. This may seem unreal to you at first but it will help release your attachment to seeing this person in a negative light. It frees your energy to flow in the present with love and it connects you back to your deep core where your truth is love.

3 Think of someone to whom you would like to say something but find it difficult to communicate your feelings. See them in your mind's eye and, looking at them, allow yourself to say whatever you want to share with them about what you are feeling. Communicate how you are truly feeling to them. Let your words be clear, positive and as intense as you need them to be in order to communicate what you wish to say.

4 Now visualize someone with whom you are angry. Holding their image in your mind's eye, let yourself say clearly and directly how you feel. After you have done this take a deep breath and let your feelings go. Find your tranquil center and begin to relax. As long as you are clear about what you want to say to others you will hold that intention in your energy. It will be experienced by others and may come back to you through their willingness to communicate with you.

## The Myth Of The Communicator Archetype

Each culture has its own myths about what can and cannot be communicated. Few of us dare truly express our anger, negativity or even joy openly. But, if you want to be empowered, then it is important to learn how to express yourself and say what you feel. It is as important to make yourself understood as it is to be understanding of others. Many people wish they could say what they feel but lack confidence or are afraid they will be rejected if they express themselves.

Trusting that what you have to say is valuable is good for your spiritual growth and psychological development. If you believe in your worth than your words will convey that energy and facilitate your ability to share your feelings. You may experience yourself in a totally new way when you dare to speak up about how you feel.

Unfortunately many people equate communication with meaningless exchanges like complaints, gossip and slander. These actually damage your energy field, particularly the Throat chakra. They can also leave you feeling depressed and drained. To keep your spirits uplifted it is important to be positive and affirming in what you say and what you hear. There is so much negativity in communication so it is worth while being discerning about what you expose yourself to.

Learning to communicate what is bothering you, without making it significant, frees you from any attachment you may have to your feelings. When you can state simply what you are feeling then you are not holding on to your emotions or making them more significant than they are. As you express positive feelings you'll enjoy the flow of energy which goes with being affirmative. Clear communication doesn't have to be always serious and intense; it can be the truth simply stated. And sometimes it can even be quite funny and light hearted.

## MEDITATION

Sit in a comfortable position, with your back straight and your neck and jaw relaxed and free. Take several deep breaths and release your jaw. Let it be free as you take the air in through your nose and slowly release it out through your mouth. As you free the muscles in your neck let your tongue relax and gently fall towards the back of your throat.

Visualize an inverted pyramid with a shining blue light radiating down in the center of your Throat chakra. This pyramid lights up your mouth and jaw, your nose and throat. It frees tension in your vocal chords and at the back of your neck. See this energy strengthening your Throat chakra so that you are able to concentrate energy in this area. As you breathe and release tension you can now say what you need to communicate to others. Allow yourself to feel that you are completely understood and don't have to struggle to say what you feel.

Your words come easily and express your clearest thoughts and deepest feelings. Know that you have a right to speak up and that others do listen to you. Your words are now an expression of a deeper, more harmonious level of awareness within you.

As you bring your awareness back to the outer world sit in silence for a moment and feel your inner reality and connect it with feeling the world around you. Be still in silence for as long as you are comfortable.

## Vitality

The Throat chakra discharges excess energy lodged in the body which needs to be released. You can release some excess energy by saying words such as NO and YES to release pent-up aggression and frustration. These words can represent the feelings from an entire range of situations you have been in where you didn't express yourself. Often the words stay stuck inside until you feel able to free them up.

You can vitalize your Throat chakra by lying on your back on a warm, but firm, surface. Put your knees up and rest the palms of your hands on your belly as you take a deep breath in and release your breath slowly out through your mouth. Allow a sound to come up from deep in your pelvis. Play with different pitches and qualities of the sounds you are making. So often we are mute when we are happy as well as when we are sad. Let this be a joyful exercise as you play with sound.

As you release the sounds from your throat, imagine they have a color and that you are actually painting with sound. This will let you make rich blends of noises and harmonies. You will feel relaxed and energized at the end of this exercise, with a more open and expressive Throat chakra.

You can also try the following.

Reciting a poem out loud

Inviting friends around for an evening of telling funny stories or jokes

Singing folksongs or your favorite TV theme tunes

Sharing life stories with trusted friends

Learning to trust your perceptions of others and keeping a journal of first impressions

## Empowerment

When you express your truth you feel good about yourself and your communication is joyful and full of positive energy. When someone is depressed noticed how their voice sounds flat and lifeless.

To empower yourself you need to be willing to take risks with how you express yourself. The more you hold on to your feelings the more congested and tight your actual vocal apparatus becomes. Saying the following affirmations out loud lets you experiment with being playful, serious, funny, angry or sad. Be willing to act the clown and enjoy expressing yourself in a new way.

*I speak up for myself.*

*Others value what I have to say.*

*I listen to my inner voice.*

*I am entitled to express my feelings.*

*I speak from my heart.*

*I listen to my feelings and express them in an appropriate way.*

*I speak my truth and I allow others to speak theirs.*

*I trust in the integrity of my words.*

*As I express myself I open my creativity.*

*I select my words with care and love.*

*My voice is powerful and reflects the depths of my inner being.*

*I am developing my integrity every time I speak my truth.*

*I know that I am love and that as I express myself my beauty shines.*

## Case Histories

### Lorraine

Lorraine is a homeopathic doctor in her early forties who suffered an accident several years ago and seriously damaged her throat. She was told she might never be able to speak again. She underwent several painful operations and, finally, with great effort and considerable willpower, managed to partially regain the use of her voice. She suffered a great deal of pain through the ordeals of surgery and yet managed to internalize her compassion to such a degree that anyone who is around her feels instantly uplifted by her presence. She is committed to working with others in a healing capacity, and brings such a degree of intention and light into her consulting room that people feel better before they have even told her their problems. When I met her, I had the experience, perhaps for the first time in my life, of being truly understood. I realized what a rare and unusual experience this was, even among other homeopaths. I am sure that this quality of understanding others is a function of her intent to be present in her communication and to provide the space for others to express themselves to the best of their ability. Because speaking requires such hard work on her part, she must focus her intention. Whatever she has had to say to me has been taken in and assimilated because I value her wisdom and the effort it has taken her to communicate with me.

She does not waste energy on superficial talk nor does she allow herself to be negative about her infirmity. She represents the true Communicator

archetype, both in her ability to say what she means and in her receptivity
to the communications of others.

## *Andy*

Andy is a consultant to senior level managers in the business world. He is
in his mid-forties, holds a degree in psychology and is an active sportsman. He is also a family man who has good relations with his partner and
his children.

Nearly everyone who meets him likes him. This is because he has a
realistic and engaging manner with people. He is never bombastic, nor is he
ungrounded in what he says to others, professionally or personally. He has
the ability to make room for others to express their feelings and, when he
feels that he has a receptive audience, he enjoys expressing his inner truths.

He loves music and often will play a beautiful song, rich in feeling, to
express a special moment. There is a richness and quality to time spent
with him, he is not afraid of silence nor is he timid about a good laugh.
When he is uncertain or doesn't know something, he will say so and he is
not ashamed to express his vulnerability when he feels tired or low.

Knowing him for several years has given me a great respect for his
way of being in the world. I know that he continues to evolve and
develop, which always makes him interesting to be around, and I value his
real and congruent communication. Through his ability to communicate
with integrity he has helped many people find their truth and heal that part
of themselves which has been silent and wounded. The balance between
his clear communication and his willingness to stand up for himself makes
him a valuable person to those he works with and those who are fortunate
to be his friends.

# 8

# THE BROW CHAKRA
Wisdom, knowledge, intuition, discernment, and imagination

DYSFUNCTIONAL ARCHETYPE:
*The Intellectual*

FUNCTIONAL ARCHETYPE:
*The Intuitive*

## HOW THE BROW CHAKRA FUNCTIONS

The Brow chakra is known as the control center of the body because it is from here that conscious control is mobilized for our physical, emotional and mental well-being. It is the center for thinking, analysis, discernment, intuition and wisdom. It is also the seat of psychic and artistic gifts, and where the heights of our imagination can inspire us.

As we focus our awareness in this center we open to the Higher Self that part of us which connects with the spiritual realms. It is from here we receive uplifting ideas which give us a sense of virtue and ethics. The Higher Self serves our conscious awareness as a guide and protector as we deal with the uncertainties of life.

A balanced Brow center combines a clearly focused left brain, which computes and analyzes, and an open right brain which is where our intuitive, artistic and psychic gifts reside. Concentrating on this center teaches us discernment and wisdom. We can focus on our inner state of awareness and on the outer world around us at the same time. It helps us see clearly what is important for our well-being and happiness, and gives us a sense of perspective as well as insight.

When something is right for us our inner knowing tells us. When we worry or get caught up in endless mental complexities we are stressing the Brow chakra. It can be a beacon of light for our healing and development when we open this center. We misuse the energy from it when we manipulate our environment or others in an attempt to control life. Meditation can be both calming and centering for the Brow chakra.

The two archetypes which reflect the energy from this center are the Intellectual which represents the over-burdened intellectualization of the Brow center and the Intuitive which epitomizes the open right brain available to enhance our sense of pleasure, as well as the world of beauty, color and the mysterious realm of the spirit.

## *Dysfunctional Archetype: The Intellectual*

### Recognizing The Intellectual

When the Brow chakra is dysfunctional it is generally from an over-intellectualization about life. This means that the intellectual gifts are not being used as they were meant to be, which is as a means of understanding and solving the problems in our life.

If we feel stupid and unable to think for ourselves we may fall into the right brain without developing our mental gifts fully. Doubt and confusion can stop us from fully developing our minds as well. If we are living too much in our left brain we will be reliant on plans, maps and future outcomes to control our lives. If we are living too much in the right brain we will only be living in the *now* without concern for our future. The Intellectual archetype theorizes about everything rather than being dynamically in tune with the cycles of energy around it. Thus it represents a real imbalance and misuse of our thinking capabilities.

This archetype tries to master the forces of chaos by living from the dictates and constrictions of the left brain only and it seldom engages with its feelings, particularly those surrounding fear and insecurity.

The Intellectual suppresses its feelings, which may be highly irrational, rather than be faced with experiencing overwhelming emotions that make it feel out of control in response to situations. Its mind is dry and has a static quality to it which limits its happiness and restricts its capacity for joy. While it attempts to control its world it avoids having to listen to its inner voice which may be saying that it is time to relax, enjoy the day or smell the roses.

The Intellectual is also highly opinionated and has many ideas based on information from secondary sources, rather than trusting what comes from its direct experience. It does not trust its own intuition to provide a valuable source of information to guide it through life's challenges or uncertainties.

The Intellectual has an over-stimulated mind and is often full of tension from worrying or thinking too much. It constantly relies on habitual or mechanical responses to new situations which limit its possibilities for expansion. It feels safe responding in the old, familiar patterns which eliminate having to confront doubts, fears or confusion. Chaos is a part of reality and developing a way of incorporating it into our lives is part of growth. When we are able to adapt to the changes of life and, at the same time, be grounded in ourselves, we can experience life as a flowing and profoundly mysterious event rather than as rigid, mechanical and fixed. Having a philosophy based on the value of personal experience and inner knowing gives us healthy and grounded ways of responding to life while embracing our wholeness and respecting our individuality.

The Intellectual rationalizes, intellectualizes and theorizes its way through life, seldom trusting its feelings or seeking guidance from within. As this archetype stays stuck in the realm of ideas and concepts its energy stagnates and atrophies, and the more it programs control into its life, the less margin it has for peace and ease. It is always striving to achieve, gain and conquer. This is exhausting and leaves it tired, anxious and preoccupied.

When we only live from the dictates of our left brain, the realm of rational thinking and computing, we miss the other half of life that is so rich in joy. There is a whole universe of imagination, intuition and wisdom waiting to be balanced with our intellectual capacities. True balance requires an acceptance of the unknown and the realm of the spontaneous to match the fixed ideas and patterns of the Intellectual's life.

### Beginning to change the Intellectual mentality

If the Intellectual avoids this source of available energy and aliveness which exists within itself it will eventually dry up and reduce its life to predictable outcomes. Balance means tempering theory with living and finding a blend of thoughts and feelings. The Intellectual gets caught up in the world of ideas, afraid to experience itself in new and dynamic ways. Given the opportunity for growth and exploration it will decline to shift its attitudes and will remain stuck in the rarefied world of words, concepts and plans.

It can destroy its health and undermine its emotional connections to people by remaining in this archetype. The Intellectual needs grounding in the warmth of personal relationships and the pleasure of its body. It needs to reconnect with the earth element and feel itself in life.

# MOVING ON FROM THE INTELLECTUAL

## Taking Responsibility For Yourself

We all have the capacity to use our minds to heal our lives and create happiness for ourselves. Our lives are fuller and richer when we can bring our intelligence into play with our feelings. This helps us develop a fuller capacity to discern what is good for us and to be happy about ourselves. Our intelligence is enriched when we use our intuition and imagination to help us distill wisdom from our life's experience and to create the future the way we would like it to be.

Taking responsibility for ourselves means that we open our minds to the many ways we can access information. In order to think for ourselves, we need to use all of our faculties to know what and who is for our highest good and greatest joy.

Being able to think clearly is important; it is the natural balance to allowing our feelings the space to blossom and not overreact when we have a problem. Proper use of the intellect is finding a balanced and holistic way of managing in life. It is only a tool we have been given. We need to know when and how to use it. When we put the intellect in the service of the spirit we find a way of developing wisdom, discernment and other noble qualities which carry us through life's crises and sustain us.

## Exercise

This exercise is to help you use both hemispheres of your brain. It employs two different ways of looking at a person or situation so that you can see how you use the different functions of your brain to solve a problem or gain insight.

**1** Take a situation or a person in your life and access your thoughts and feelings about them.

**2** What are your thoughts about this situation or person? Your thoughts may be something like: "I think that John is immature and difficult. If he would be willing to take in my point of view, we might get along better."

**3** Now ask yourself what your feelings are. If you do not get a clear sense of your feelings you might try using colored pens to represent your feelings and shapes to help you describe the situation or person. Your right brain responds easily to metaphors, symbols and colors.

**4** If your thoughts and your intuition give you different information about this person or situation, which are you going to trust? Are you going to listen to your mind? Or are you going to trust your feelings and intuition? You may wish to ask yourself which function gives you the most reliable picture, your thoughts or your feelings?

This exercise helps you understand your own intellectual processes. Use this technique whenever you want to evaluate an experience. It is a balanced and reliable way to trust your ability to discern the nature of a person or situation. You may be wrong at times, but if you want to develop your intuition you may have to make some mistakes. The more you can relax the more your intuition will flow freely.

## The Myth Of The Intellectual Archetype

The saddest myths are about people who believe they need to be perfect and who never achieve their dreams. They live from an idea which doesn't encompass either mistakes, inconsistencies or imperfections. As a consequence they suffer and do not trust life to provide the good things they need.

So often people who primarily inhabit the left hemisphere of the brain, and ignore the right hemisphere, do so because their feelings were ignored when they were children. Ignoring a child's needs and feelings is damaging because it forces it to live in the inner realms of its mind, never trusting its feelings or intuition.

How strongly do you live in your mind? Are you ready to open yourself to your inner strengths and powers which can help you expand yourself? Trusting yourself and loving life, take courage and, at times, this may mean going against what others feel is right or even what society says is right.

When you trust yourself, you begin to live by an inner set of rules which are consistent with universal laws. These laws are ancient and have guided men and women for generations through the pathways of life to realize their own worth and beauty as spiritual beings. They are life enhancing and totally supportive of the good.

Be willing to give some attention to your intuition. You may wish to take up a class or course which will open up your intuition or the inner world of the imagination. This will help you feel grounded and comfortable in this new territory of your mind. Learn to trust your intuition. It will help you find your inner wisdom. You have all the answers within you. It is time to access the depths of your experiences which you have been gathering from lifetimes of learning. It will help you develop your own philosophy of life. The best any spiritual teaching can offer you is the capacity to develop your own inner knowing.

# MEDITATION

Sit in a comfortable position and begin to relax, taking several deep breaths in through your nose and releasing them out through your mouth.

As you begin to relax imagine a beautiful flower. Let this represent your inner nature.

Now visualize a tree which you feel best represents your strength and willpower.

Finally, visualize an animal which you feel symbolizes your physical energy.

Gently bring your consciousness back into the present.

The flower describes your emotional nature, the tree describes your spiritual strength and the animal represents your physical vitality. Reflect on the qualities of these symbols and use your intuition to grasp the inner essence of your personality which these represent. You may wish to draw or find pictures of these symbols to act as a reminder of your inner beauty.

## Vitality

An instant way of getting more vitality in your life is to use your mind to release any negative thoughts you are holding on to. You can do this while on the move or standing still. The more negative thoughts you let go of the more your vitality will flow.

Negativity has a weight to it which you carry around in your energy field. Be patient and watch as your energy levels rise and you stimulate your life force to move in a positive direction by releasing negative thoughts.

Practice letting go of heavy or uncomfortable situations from your mind. It is often good to ask yourself if you really need the weight of this problem or the resentment you feel to be carried around at this moment in time. When you begin to understand how responsive your vitality is to positive and negative thoughts you will let go of what you don't want to carry any longer.

Other suggestions include the following.

Learning to relax

Taking up some form of exercise which could include stretching or simple movement to music

Doing childish things such as walking in puddles or fingerpainting

Listening to music

## Empowerment

You empower yourself whenever you acknowledge that you are doing the right thing for yourself in any situation. We are all limited by the negativity within the collective unconscious, no matter how much we affirm that we want joy, love and light in our lives. History, collective negativity and our own limited awareness of the cosmic purpose hold us back from being positive all the time. You empower yourself when you are gentle and kind to yourself and look within to understand what your heart's desire is. Try saying the following affirmations looking into a mirror or out loud. You will gather to you a greater sense of your own power.

*I forgive myself for my own limitations.*

*I always do the best I can in any situation.*

*I listen to my inner voice and let it guide me to peace and happiness.*

*I love and trust that my life is unfolding as it should.*

*I acknowledge that I am perfect in myself.*

*I give over my negativity to my soft and gentle feelings.*

*I integrate the light and shadowy sides of myself by giving my negativity space to be and then letting it go.*

*I look inside and listen to the messages which guide and protect me.*

*I open to my intuition and trust that goodness is mine.*

*I am wise.*

*I tap into my inner wisdom and know that all is well in my world.*

*I open my imagination to create the best of all possible worlds for myself.*

## Case Histories

### Marla

Marla is a woman in her late forties. She is extremely intelligent and has degrees from two major universities and qualifications which are numerous and impressive. She prides herself on being able to converse on a variety of subjects with some authority and speaks four languages.

She encourages her children to strive for success in school and rewards them if they do well with affection and presents. She places so much emphasis on intellectual achievement and has said to her children that the only thing she cannot tolerate is stupidity. She is constantly criticizing others for not being good enough and there is a strong sense about her that she knows best about what is right and correct. She is also very competitive and eager to win, often at the expense of hurting others. She has planned her life very carefully and programs her time so that she manages to have very limited contact with just a few people. Her marriage is stale and love-less, and her relationship with her children is cold and full of fear.

It began to dawn on her how isolated she had become. Her old patterns of distancing and isolating herself were evident to her, but she didn't know how to put her life back on track. She was willing to try group workshops, homeopathy and other holistic approaches to heal her tendency to control life, and as she had recently begun to develop a painful health condition, she felt some of these options were worth trying.

She was so uncomfortable with her physical health problems that, for the first time in many years, she wept from the pain. It was the only time she had any relief. She began to take her feelings into account and an inner voice emerged from within her which directed her to be softer and more open to others. She realized that she needed to have access to her feelings, and be able to reach out to her friends and family.

She used her intelligence to understand what price her haughty attitudes had cost her in regard to her feelings and her happiness. Her willingness to become a free and more open person was genuine, and as she developed in herself and was more in touch with her own emotional reality, her health problems began to ease up. She used her intellect to understand the theory of suppression, for instance, and knew that she had locked away her feelings and had been living in her mind for a very long time. It wasn't easy for her to look at her pain and to experience her feelings.

As she eventually gave over the strict control of her emotions she found herself having more vitality and more intimate contact with others. This was the payoff for her and her levels of well-being continued to increase as she felt well more frequently. She is developing a more balanced way of life and enjoying herself for the first time in many years. As she is less critical and is more supportive of others, she finds people reaching out to her in more genuinely caring ways. This has touched her deeply and has given her a chance to live a more balanced life.

---

### *Antony*

---

Antony is a well-educated, upper middle-class man in his early fifties who achieved distinction at the university and eventually took over his father's business. He was given little warmth or affection in his childhood and was sent away to boarding school at an early age to be regimented and processed, as members of his class and family had been for generations.

He had the good fortune to fall in love and marry a warm-hearted and caring woman who, for many years, provided the nurturing and sustenance that had been missing in his early life. His marriage eventually started to become shaky when his wife pleaded for some tenderness and affection from him. He was stunned by this demand on him because, in his experience, he only knew how to live from his intellect and had little awareness of how to respond openly from his feelings. He was very dry and rigid.

This was the most painful crisis of his life and sent him into a deep depression which lasted for months. He went for therapy and homeopathy to help him. His wife agreed to stay with him in the hope that he could open up and become the loving man she felt he was capable of becoming. Fortunately he was intelligent enough to realize that only he was responsible for his capacity to love. He wept for the lost love he missed as a child and he developed a compassionate nature which grew into a rich spiritual awareness as he matured. He found the balance between his intellect and his feelings. His marriage endured and became a source of intimacy for both him and his wife.

## *Functional Archetype: The Intuitive*

---

### Recognizing The Intuitive

As we transcend the Intellectual archetype we move towards accessing our deepest knowing which we call our intuition. When we live from the depths of self we become wise. We can make choices for ourselves and help others to find their inner wisdom. Native Americans call this *the time of the grandparents*. Traditionally it was the elders of a tribe or community who pooled their wisdom to guide the families under their care. In our time this tradition has been lost and we are left to find our own inner wisdom for building sane and healthy lives.

This highly developed archetype has the gift of inner sight, known as clairvoyance, and trusts in its inner knowing to provide guidance and answers to life's perplexities. It offers protection for itself and others through following the guidance its inner vision provides.

To live from that place of deep trust requires an impeccable sense of trust and love for life to know that it will see you through painful and difficult times. The Intuitive archetype has both these qualities as well as patience and faith.

It has a basic belief in the benign nature of the universe and it knows everything holds within it the full potential for goodness and love. This philosophy is the guiding light of its life. The Intuitive uses the gift of insight and wisdom to enhance its life and to serve others with its awareness. It is open to positive forces working for the happiness and well-being of the greater whole because it knows that no one ever succeeds alone. We are all part of a greater whole and this knowledge guides the Intuitive in serving higher consciousness and spiritual awareness. It trusts that all experience is ultimately for the highest good, even if it is, during the interim, painful and difficult.

The Intuitive knows about the necessity of experiencing change and sometimes the terrible emotional stress that accompanies it in order for people to grow. It accepts that this is part of the process of change.

Today many people are developing their intuitive skills. As our sensitivity increases we are better able to cope with events in our lives and to understand the nature of the changes we undergo. If our gifts are used in the service of others as well as for our personal happiness we gain a stronger trust in the Source. True intuitives are gracious people who know that there is always enough of everything we need and that lack is a concept maintained through doubt and negative thinking.

The Intuitive archetype has a deep understanding of the inner core of life and how people, who are not in touch with that core can be lost in the web of their illusions. It knows that things are not always what they appear to be on the surface and it accepts both the fragility and strength of human nature. It knows that limitation is a part of the natural process of development and at the same time it encourages everyone to be positive and develop their full potential. The Intuitive is a loving and supportive contributor to everyone's well-being.

The Intuitive archetype makes a wonderful therapist, healer, artist or actor. It works from that part of the brain which understands metaphor and symbols and, as part of its psychic development, it becomes skilled at interpreting these symbols. It knows, for instance, what is at the heart of things. This is called second sight or inner vision and it connects this archetype to the world of the invisible, the realm of spirit.

The subconscious mind is the direct link to our spirit. Our growth processes are directly linked with its metaphoric content to give us both inner guidance and wisdom. The Intuitive listens to its messages and knows that the voice which projects these metaphors must be honored and listened to. It accepts the inner workings of the subconscious as valid information useful for its healing.

This archetype accepts everyone on the planet has lessons to learn. The Intuitive uses its imagination and intuitive skill to guide others through difficult or challenging times. It pays attention to the messages of dreams and sees inner processes unfold through the symbolic content of these dreams. It pays attention to the images which the subconscious mind releases to be decoded so that we can understand and follow its guidance.

Nature gives the Intuitive its symbols to the inner process of the mind and offers guidance to traverse the world we call reality. The natural world represents the perfect mirror of the unconscious mind and the Intuitive knows this and lives life accordingly, never blaming and always accepting that everything serves conscious unfoldment. Its work is to interpret these symbols into messages and pay attention to the signals that come through.

The Intuitive never discounts synchronicity or coincidence and fully understands the power of the mind to create the experience the spirit needs for its growth. The Intuitive knows thoughts are powerful and creative and it draws experiences to it like magnets. The Intuitive understands the inner creative process and works with it to enhance the quality of life for all around it. It knows everything we need is available to us to enhance our development. It is aware too that inner peace and serenity come with acceptance and are not to be obtained in the external world. This is, in truth, a state of mind.

### The thriving Intuitive

The Intuitive archetype has always thrived in cultures which have honored the need of the human spirit to express its inner connection with universal forces. It is recognized today by spiritual cultures who revere life as sacred and who honor the Source. For instance, the Oracle of the Tibetan Buddhist is used by the Dalai Lama as a sacred vessel which channels Divine Wisdom. In Native American tribes, Polynesian religions and Eastern cultures the Intuitive is deeply respected and honored. It is acknowledged that they see through the veil of our limited minds and have the ability to connect us with the power and mystery of the eternal.

We are beginning in the West to look again for this lost function to enrich and expand our lives and to help us understand our place in the universe. Everyone has the ability to open themselves to this part of their mind if they wish to do so. It is a skill which can be developed and it offers the individual who chooses its path the delights and wonder of the powerful mystery we call life.

# DEVELOPING THE INTUITIVE

## Taking Responsibility For Yourself

We are all capable of opening our intuition to higher degrees of perception and knowing. When we begin to trust ourselves our lives are transformed into a magical quest for deeper connections into the beauty and mystery of spirit. To live fully from that place requires that we develop a special relationship with our inner nature. The foundation of this is based on loving and accepting ourselves as we are and knowing we are worthy of kindness, gentleness and serenity in our lives. It is also accepting that the universe is a benign and loving place.

The more we love and honor ourselves the more deeply in touch we become with our spirit. When we do things that make us happy we are helping our spirit to open. When we complete projects and tasks we are strengthening the integrity of our spirits and taking responsibility for ourselves. When we listen to ourselves and trust in the quality of our experience we honor ourselves.

## Exercise

You can begin to develop and strengthen your intuition by doing the exercise below.

1 Begin by making a list of ten things you would like to know about. They can be situations in your life, people or circumstances you have not understood before.

Be very still and relaxed as you go inside yourself. You may wish to spend a few moments in meditation to clear your conscious mind and to be a clean channel for your perceptions. First ask yourself what is important to you about each of these things. Ask your subconscious mind to give you pictures or symbols which you can interpret and which will tell you what you need to know about these things. For instance, you may want to know the meaning of a past relationship in your life. You may wish to know what its purpose was for you and what it was meant to teach you about yourself. You may be hard pressed to see the learning or the good in a difficult or painful situation. You may need to release your negative feelings about it before awareness can come to you. Breathe and relax as you wait for whatever messages or pictures come into your mind's eye. You can write this information down in a journal or notebook. Look inside yourself to know if what you receive feels right. From time to time this is a good technique to use for expanding your understanding of events and people in your life.

2  You can go inside yourself to check out whether something feels right or not for you. Be still and tune in to yourself. If you are holding any tension feel it and ask yourself what memory or emotion is lodged in your body. It may be a deposit of tensions related to old attitudes you are holding on to. When you get an answer take a breath and release your tension. If the tension stays lodged in your body you may need to ask yourself what is blocked. Is it anger? Is it sadness? What does it relate to and what is it you need to realize before you are free of this tension? The answer is always within you so ask yourself what this issue is about. Life can be so simple when you feel what you need to feel and affirm yourself with love and gentleness.

## The Myth Of The Intuitive Archetype

We all have intuition and are capable of knowing everything that is happening anywhere in the universe at any moment. We are only limited by our belief that life must be regulated and controlled by certain habits, conditions, boundaries and rules, and the belief that we are innocent bystanders letting things happen to us at random. Trusting our intuition opens the doors to our knowing.

Most of us live contained within the limits of our mind and by what our families, churches and educational institutes tell us is true. Occasionally we release the rules for a brief moment and we get a glimpse of what is possible when we expand our consciousness and grasp the magnificence and splendor of the universe. Sometimes it takes a willingness to say to yourself: "I am open to all the possibilities that exist beyond my limited knowledge."

When we expand our minds to include the wonders and magic of the universe a special awareness begins to unfold for us. Be willing to release your limitations and expand your awareness about what may be possible in your life. This way you can walk the path of your destiny and be in touch with the full potential God has given you. Everything you do is meant to enhance your spirit and help you come to know and understand the magnificence of who you are.

## MEDITATION

Sit comfortably and take some deep breaths. As you drift into a meditative state allow yourself to imagine your life as you would truly like it to be. You may wish to see yourself walking in a beautiful place in nature surrounded by a group of people or a person you deeply love. It may be a friend or a lover, or a group of people you feel strongly connected with. Feel relaxed and comfortable with yourself. If you don't know anyone whom you feel you would like to be with then imagine that there is someone you can feel completely at one with and whom it is a pleasure to be with.

Imagine that you feel happy, healthy and fit. You feel loved and supported by everyone around you. You know you have everything you need to be fulfilled. There is enough love, support and money to do the things you enjoy. You have the time and energy to complete everything you want in life. You are thankful for all the good in your life. If there is anything you need you can create it with your imagination now in your meditation. Let yourself feel deeply satisfied and happy.

The more positive your attitude to life is the more happiness and joy you will manifest around you. This will help you heal and at the same time will allow those around you to heal.

## Vitality

Using your mind to create what you want can be part and parcel of your development. Making sure that you have access to all the energy you need to enjoy what you want from life is essential. To give yourself the vitality you require you may need to look at your life in a different way.

What are you doing that takes most of your energy?

Are you working too hard?

Do you spend all your time looking after others?

Are you studying for a course?

Do you fight with your partner or boss?

Why are you not doing what you love and enjoy the most?

Whatever it is that saps your vitality needs to be re-evaluated in the light of your personal happiness so that you can have the energy you need to enjoy your life. If you are giving your life force to your work, relationship or projects and there isn't enough left over for you it is time to redress the balance. You may need to ask yourself if you are doing too much for others rather than for yourself. Ask yourself if you are allowed to enjoy some energy for your well-being and happiness. If you have a problem here it is time to look at how you use your energy.

Make a list of the things that are important to your well-being. Also look at the following suggestions and see what you could be doing to enhance your life.

Visiting your family and friends

Making more time for your social life

Taking more exercise

Reading spiritually uplifting books

Taking time each day to communicate with your Creator

Being thankful for the good in your life

## Empowerment

In order to empower yourself use your intuitive gifts to give yourself both the acknowledgement and peace you need to feel good about yourself. Knowing that you are doing the best for yourself helps you feel good about yourself. Say these affirmations in front of a mirror or out loud so that you can integrate them into your vision of life.

*I live, love and am creative.*

*What I do for myself is to love and honor who I am right now.*

*I am open to my highest awareness and listen.*

*I receive guidance and protection at all times.*

*My awareness increases as I tune into my inner knowing.*

*The goodness and abundance of the universe is available to me at all times.*

*Life always offers me an opportunity for growth and development.*

*I am learning with every experience I have that I am a valuable and lovable being.*

*I am learning to discern what is for my highest good and greatest joy.*

*Life is a beautiful experience full of love and joy.*

*I am happy to be still and listen carefully to my inner voice.*

*I have nothing to prove in life. I am free to do what gives me joy and happiness.*

# Case Histories

## *Alexandra*

Alexandra is a young and talented American woman who is deeply intuitive and highly clairvoyant. Unlike many psychics, she has explored and used her gifts to generate a happy, healthy and fulfilled life for herself. Clear about her power and true to her integrity, she assists thousands of people every year to realize their full potential.

Alexandra has an Institute for Psychic Development in California and teaches people to develop their own intuitive talents. I first met her when a friend invited me to an introductory evening class. Alexandra went around the room offering each person some information about themselves. She told me two things which I could not believe at the time. She told me I would change my name and that I would move to a cold climate to live and work. Four years later, I had changed my name and moved to England, to Manchester, to pursue my homeopathic studies.

Several years after my first meeting with Alexandra, I went to see her on discovering that my sister was going to have a bone marrow transplant. I wanted to know if she would live through the ordeal. Alexandra told me many things in that reading, but wouldn't answer that particular question. She just said, "Be sure to tell your sister that you love her." These turned out to be the last words I spoke to my sister.

A few years later while I was visiting California, she told me interesting and wonderful things which subsequently unfolded just as she said they would.

What is so exceptional about Alexandra is the beauty and grace with which she offers her intuition. Every day there are long lines of people at her center waiting to see her. She helps them all. She is neither bombastic, nor seeking to make herself look important. She runs her Institute along sound educational and business guidelines. She is a wise woman who has learned to honor her gifts by developing herself fully and now teaches others how to do the same. She has been a source of guidance and help for me and many others.

## Stephen Levine

Stephen Levine is a writer and a poet whose works I have read for many years and thoroughly enjoyed. He has, in recent years, come to work with the sick and dying; offering comfort, solace and release from emotional suffering. He has brought a spiritual dimension to people's lives which has helped so many find their hearts and reconnect with their souls before dying. His work is highly intuitive, and his love and trust in the Source is confirmed every day in the reality of his work. Only someone with great faith in the workings of Divine Grace would be as open and trusting in the face of death as he is. He helped me open my heart to the goodness and the love in the universe through his books, articles and lectures. His spirit is joyful and his wisdom deep. His work is intuitive and, at the same time, grounded. He follows his heart, which has given him the strength and fortitude he needs in dealing with something most people in our culture cannot come to terms with. Although I do not know him, his work has directly inspired me to trust and love the Source in myself. For that reason he is the best example I know of a male Intuitive.

# 9

# THE CROWN CHAKRA
Beauty, spirituality, connection with the Divine Source

DYSFUNCTIONAL ARCHETYPE:
*The Egotist*

FUNCTIONAL ARCHETYPE:
*The Guru*

## HOW THE CROWN CHAKRA FUNCTIONS

The Crown chakra embodies the summit of beauty, refinement and spirituality that we can experience in our lives. The function of the Crown chakra is to open us to the light of spirit which is eternally connected to the Source. Each of us can look within ourselves to this point of connection where we are one with the Source. The Crown chakra channels the energy of that part of ourselves, often called the Higher Self, and embraces us within its healing and protective light. In this place there is always joy and an abiding sense of peace.

When we are open to receiving the love and wisdom from our Higher Self we are filled with the energy of the Divine, guiding and inspiring us in all we do. At this level of awareness we walk the path of destiny, touching life from the center outward.

The two archetypes which represent the functional and dysfunctional aspects of the Crown chakra are the Egotist and the Guru. The Egotist is the narcissistic personality which is boastful and ungrateful. The Guru, on the other hand, acknowledges the Divine Source and knows that all things come from the grace of the Higher Self within. There is a vast qualitative difference in energy and awareness between the arrogance of the one and the wisdom of the other.

# *Dysfunctional Archetype: The Egotist*

## Recognizing The Egotist

When the Crown chakra is closed we experience an archetype which, because of the high degree of conscious development and success it has in the world, is often resistant to developing its spiritual awareness. It can be described as proud, arrogant and full of its own self importance. The Egotist is stuck at a level of self gratification, which can be defined in psychological terms as narcissism or, more specifically, a grandiose false self separate from the true core. The Egotist is rooted in the belief that only it is responsible for its personal achievements in life. This is completely opposite to the Victim archetype, which feels that everyone else is responsible for its life.

The Egotist stubbornly refuses any interest in spirituality or even acknowledging the presence of a guiding and protecting presence in its life. It is convinced that everything is within its control. Its arrogance prevents it from being humble or for asking for help from others when it needs support or cannot find true peace with itself.

The Egotist does not acknowledge the power or presence of anyone or anything higher than itself. Nor does it want to understand that spirit is the bedrock upon which the ego flourishes in a healthy person. The Egotist believes that nothing has the ability to directly influence its life except its own course of action. Often all focus and activity is centered in the left brain, the conscious, rational mind. The Egotist sees itself as the sole cause of its experience. It rejects other people for their imperfections and is often very lonely and isolated. The Egotist can be a highly conscious person with a well-developed intuition. It is capable of being very creative, reliable and highly productive. But it feels it has no need to acknowledge a higher force within as it thinks of its personality, or false self, as the highest force possible. It doesn't open to the spiritual part of itself, but relies on the ego as its greatest strength. This represents its limitation to spiritual growth and awareness.

The Egotist is very entrenched in the material world and has a vision of life which is mechanical in the extreme. It believes in harsh approaches to dealing with the body when it is ill or in pain, and it easily disregards the emotions as a sign of weakness. It can be punishing to itself and others as a means of expressing its disapproval. It imposes its will on everything it can control. It doesn't put its faith in God, or the Higher Self, nor is it aware of the goodness and sweetness of life. It lives a very separate existence without any sense of the Oneness of the Universe. There is no depth to the Egotist, everything is on the surface and externalized out into the world.

The Egotist can enjoy refuting evidence that spirit is the guiding light in humanity. It can reach old age and still resist any other view of life than that one which defines humankind as supreme. Its Crown chakra will remain closed until the last moment of its life. Its perceptions will limit it and hold it back from its own evolution.

It is spirit alone which imbues the life force. The Egotist thinks and feels it has all the power it needs and that its energy alone can solve its problems. It uses sheer force and willpower to resolve issues. It separates itself off from the higher spheres of awareness by believing in its own omnipotence. It fails to understand that, at core, we exist with the help and co-operation of higher spiritual guidance and can call upon that realm of energy and awareness for help and assistance at any time.

## MOVING ON FROM THE EGOTIST

### Taking Responsibility For Yourself

Living from our deepest knowing and realizing that, at core, each of us is an aspect of God, is ultimately taking responsibility for who we are. We are all aspects of the Source. To open up to our Divine nature is to permit our spirit to shine with joy and radiance in the world. One way to do this is to let go of the ego identifications you are attached to and which give you a false sense of yourself.

When we identify with anything outside of self as being more important than our spirit, we diminish ourselves. We may think that who we are is a body in male or female form, a mother or father, healer or patient. We may choose to identify with our professional status or economic wealth when, in fact, we are not any of these things. Whatever we chose to identify with is only an aspect of the persona or mask which the spirit chooses to embody within.

### Exercise

1 Be willing to take a serious look at your ego identifications. Whom and what do you identify with? Are you identified with your sex, nationality, economic status, education or profession? Do you experience yourself as something more than this? Do you see yourself as different or special?

**2** If you are not any of these ego identifications, ask yourself who you are. Give yourself the time you need to contemplate this question.

**3** As you start to identify a new sense of yourself which connects you more completely to the whole of life be clear that you are transforming your energy to the highest level of consciousness.

If you need to ground yourself in your old familiar identifications do so by talking with someone you are familiar with or by walking in familiar surroundings. This helps you to remain grounded.

Becoming enlightened can be disorienting and frightening if you are not prepared to realize that you are none of the things you had previously identified with but rather a stronger and more beautiful spirit than anything you could have previously imagined.

## The Myth Of The Egotist Archetype

We believe that we are limited by our bodies, our intelligence or our feelings and that these limitations define us. We identify ourselves by our age, color, sex and the amount of money and opportunities available to us. We learn to separate ourselves from others because of external hierarchies of evaluation and judgement. We give over our authority and power to people we feel have more knowledge and experience than we do. A limited view of life gives away the power of our true selves to others and diminishes the richness and beauty of our true self.

We will always give away our power whenever we fail to love or honor the self. Our development relies on learning that we are one with life and an essential part of the process of creation. This is called Enlightenment, being one with the Source.

Letting go of our ego identifications, both positive or negative, is essential if we are to align our awareness with cosmic consciousness.

At this level of life all is one. We are not separate from this oneness, but an integral part of it. Once we know and experience this our lives are never the same. We gain empowerment and with that our reality shifts to one of grace and beauty.

Putting this into practice in everyday life is, in essence, living the golden rule, which says that when we are kind to someone else we are also kind to ourselves and when we love others we love ourselves.

Are you willing to give up the myth of separation? Are you willing to open to being part and parcel of one fantastically dynamic and alive process called life? Only you can make this choice. You need to be willing to release your ideas about yourself and live your life. Your ideas may be based on the notion that you are better or worse than others, and that such things as race, money or education make you better or worse than others. These are the illusions which maintain your ego.

True cosmic consciousness extends to all life. It permeates the animal, plant and mineral kingdoms. We are all made of the same substance, we all contain the consciousness of life within us. When we see that we are all a part of life, we begin to treat others more lovingly and respectfully, and we offer our support and blessings to all humanity.

# MEDITATION

Sit comfortably with your spine straight and begin to relax, breathing slowly in and out. As you begin to take your attention away from the outer reality of life and focus inside yourself hold the question "Who am I?" in your mind.

This question, or Koan as it is known in Zen, is the key that unlocks the experience of your deep awareness of who you are.

You may pass through several ego identifications before you realize your Divine nature. Give yourself the opportunity to experience yourself as deeply as you can. You may go through the stages of feeling you are nothing or that you are worthless. Remember this is only an ego identification which asks to be released when you come into contact with the self; that part of you which is light, pure, beautiful and joyful.

Try to keep a mindful awareness of who you are throughout your day. When you find yourself slipping away from yourself take a moment to reconnect. Wherever you are or whatever you are doing can take you deep inside yourself.

## Vitality

The degree of vitality we can make available to ourselves when we release our ego identifications and start to reconnect with the core of our spirit can be dynamic and powerful. There are stories of people who are so completely overwhelmed by this energy, their lives are totally transformed by it.

The energy which moves up through your chakras is called the Kundalini. When it rises up from the Root chakra and hits your Crown center the impact of it is known as Shakti, or Divine Awareness. This is the primal life energy brought up into consciousness and released in spirituality. The more you can release your ego identifications the more energy is available to move through you. This energy can create miraculous healing and enables gurus and spiritual teachers to do remarkable feats. It can give you the strength to make the shifts in your life which are necessary for your growth and healing.

To increase your vitality, look in a mirror for several minutes and do the following:

Ask yourself what your own true nature is. What are you really like?

Find something beautiful about yourself

Find something graceful about yourself

Find something timid and innocent about yourself

Find something humorous about yourself

Can you see joy within your reflection?

Can you release any judgement in your face and let it soften?

Can you thank your spirit for creating you just as you are?

## Empowerment

When we are clear that we are not our ego identifications we begin to live life from our Higher Self. We live in the realm of magic and mystery as we connect to the flow of cosmic energy. We become more open in our hearts and bountiful in our spirits. The depths of our love and the capacity for our joy become expansive. We radiate strength, courage, freedom and joy to everyone around us and attract love, happiness and wonderful experiences into our lives. We are whole and complete in our love and acceptance of ourselves.

Allow yourself to grasp the significance of this awareness as you say or write down the following affirmations. They will help you connect with your deepest sense of who you are.

*I am truth, freedom, love and beauty.*

*I live in the realm of cosmic consciousness.*

*I am at one with all life.*

*I live in the awareness that we are one people, one planet.*

*I open myself to experience the depths of my being.*

*I am one with the forces of life.*

*I am at peace knowing that I am protected and guided at all times.*

*I tune my will to that of infinite intelligence.*

*I connect with the highest, clearest vibrations of love in the universe.*

*My path is made gentle and easy as I lift my spirit to the highest levels of awareness.*

*I release my limited view of myself and attune to the oneness of all life.*

*There is no separation between my love and the love in the universe; we are one.*

## Case Histories

### *Gerrard*

Gerrard is a very successful businessman in his mid sixties who has amassed a huge empire and great wealth in his business life. He is a multi-millionaire and father to several children from his first wife, who had a mental breakdown after suffering years of his domination and infidelity. His second wife has a more resilient ego, but was unable to transform his selfish and domineering patterns of behavior. Gerrard believed that there wasn't anything in life but his will to make things happen. He said he felt the evidence of this in his business and personal life. His ideas were brittle and rigid, and he held to them with vigor and tenacity.

A few years ago one of his daughters became ill with cancer, and he was deeply upset and disturbed, as any father would be. As his daughter became weaker and closer to the end, Gerrard found himself praying to the powers that be to help his daughter. He actually hoped that she might recover from the strength of his prayers alone.

When his daughter found out that her father was praying for her she asked if they could pray together. Gerrard found this very difficult at first because he was embarrassed that he might be considered weak. Eventually he relented to please his daughter. They became closer and more loving with one another as they shared their deepest hopes of her recovery.

Although she eventually died, her passing was peaceful, and Gerrard felt a real sense of harmony and love that he had never known before in his busy and tumultuous life. He had found the spirit within himself and now shares with close friends and family the story of his daughter's death, feeling assured that her spirit is well and lives on. He has opened himself to a higher dimension of life and, as a result, has been transformed. He sees life and relates to people in a completely different way now. He is more gentle and aware, and has time to listen to people. He spends his leisure time with his family enjoying the blessings of their company. His experience transformed his Egotist archetype, and he is a more open and complete person.

### Jenny

Jenny was in her early thirties when I met her. She had a life that could have been made into a film. It was fraught with adventure, travel and drama. She was born in Germany at the end of the Second World War and lived most of her young life in Africa. She tamed horses and rode in national events for many years. She had a highly developed sense of her personal power and a very strong ego. She never had any reason to surrender to a higher power other than her own. Surrender was actually an uncomfortable word to her as it was something she could never imagine doing to anyone or anything. She was a free spirit and an independent person.

After a dramatic escape from Africa with little in hand except her memories, she managed to arrive in Europe to the care of family. She retrained as a secretary and went to America where she quickly succeeded in making a life for herself. In 1989 she contracted AIDS through casual sex and was cut down in the prime of her life. She didn't know whom or where to turn to as she had no deep or close relationships. She was looked after in a hospice where she was eventually brought into contact with some very caring people who shared their spiritual beliefs with her.

She reached death's door before she realized that the drama of her life was not who she was. She came to understand and experience, in the months before she died, that she was stronger than death and that her spirit was eternal. She began to recognize her true spirituality for the first time in her life. She was an inspiration to the people who knew her in the last months of her life. Like so many young people cut down in their prime, she could have died angry and resentful. Instead she saw this as an opportunity to experience the unconditional love of God channeled through the people who loved and cared for her as she lay dying. In the months before she died, she grew in spirit and guided many other people through their passing. She became clear that we are all spirit and need to learn to live from that place within ourselves. She said that there was probably someone like her in every AIDS hospice in the world. I hope she is right.

## *Functional Archetype: The Guru*

### Recognizing The Guru

Releasing all other archetypes leaves us with the highest level of responsibility, vitality and empowerment. If you are not ready to assume this ultimate power for your life, know that it is there waiting for you when you are willing to transform yourself.

As we move into the Guru archetype, the realm of possibilities expands to the infinite and we tap into the joy and bliss of our spirit. Here we are one with the Source, we are whole and complete.

The Guru represents the archetype of mastery on the spiritual plane. At this level of reality the Guru embodies the essence of love and awareness. It is the highest archetype we can attain in our life's development. The awareness and energy this state of being brings is always high, clear and beautiful. There is no separation with this archetype between self and life. Everything and everyone is linked in a oneness which resonates with a continuous flow of universal love and consciousness. When we exist at this level we operate through the laws of attraction and discernment.

Separation, judgement and criticism of oneself are not part of this archetype. There is only oneness, acceptance and love of self, experienced as the grace of one's Divine Nature.

This archetype knows that it is the Source of all its experience and accepts conscious responsibility for every aspect of its life. It turns what has been unacceptable into acceptable, what has been dark into light and what has been hidden into what can be loved and embraced. Every experience brings the awareness that everything is to help us develop into spiritual beings.

Native Americans know this to the extent that their languages describe the workings of the Great Spirit in every word. Spirit is contained within all living things. Holy men and women throughout the ages have had this knowledge and channeled this force in their teachings and healing, hoping to unite people everywhere. Those who are sensitive may feel this connection with the Source within themselves and in others around them. Spirit resides everywhere and there is no place it is not. The Guru archetype lives from that place within itself which is one with the highest part of itself. It lives in the awareness of the totality of life, with no separation from it, and is aware that this totality sustains and nourishes all life at all times.

The Guru's identity is one with the core of this profound consciousness; it knows it is Divine Spirit incarnate. Often the Guru's work is to teach others and to help them find this awareness in themselves. The quintessential quality the Guru instills in others is to live with compassion and light and to be one with the whole of life. What the Guru signifies in the hierarchy of the archetypes is mastery. This includes mastery over the body, which we know as health; mastery over the emotions, which we experience as stability; and mastery over the mind, which we call serenity. The Guru is not seeking external power as it knows real power comes only from being one's self. At core, the Guru knows that all is love and chooses to live life expressing itself in the fullness of this awareness. From this point of consciousness comes true empowerment.

The Guru never identifies with negativity or circumstances which limit, categorize or define it. It also does not attempt to interfere with anyone else's development because it understands that everyone must learn the lessons of life for themselves, no matter how hard or painful that may be. Its very being represents a profound statement about love because it lives its life in the truth of the knowledge that love is who we are.

To be in the presence of a true master shatters all illusions of separation and helps us to let go of our mind sets about who we think we may be. The Guru archetype is a level of awareness which is available to us all when we open ourselves to the highest aspirations of love. This archetype lives who it is. It is in harmony with itself and all around it, embracing life to the fullest and radiating love to all. To the Guru there are no boundaries which separate, nor time which divides. There is only the oneness of spirit which is universal and eternal. It knows its spirit existed before time and will continue to exist after time. It accepts its body as the creation of its mind and that it has the power to cure and heal its body at will. The Guru often has enlightened deaths and finds joy in returning to spirit.

The Guru knows the purpose of life is love and that love is within one's own self. It never falters in realizing this even in the face of negativity. It knows that negativity is only fear expressed outward and that all negativity is an illusion created by the limited mind to protect and defend itself. Neither physical or emotional pain, nor rejection or humiliation can affect the Guru, because it represents the true light of spirit. It is impervious to the shadow side of human nature because it has met its own dark side and released its negativity, which it knows to be the illusion that masks the wonder and beauty of the soul.

The Guru understands the nature of people and accepts limitation as an essential aspect of growth and development. It also knows that humankind is greater than anything it thinks it is. The Guru lives in the light of Divine Love and is a perfect reflection of the glory that we are capable of when we strive for the depths and fullness of our spirit. It represents transcendence in its purest form.

## Owning Your Guru Archetype

To own your Guru archetype requires a high level of love and complete acceptance of yourself as you are. Most people would rather go to a Guru and be offered enlightenment without having to do the inner work required of them. Accepting one's self fully with total love and gratitude is an act of surrender to all that one is. It means we are greater than our limitations, more creative than our imagination and more powerful than anything around us. When we know in our hearts that the purpose of life is to manifest spirit we are free to be ourselves.

Our deepest spiritual nature is love and our acceptance of that inner light may be our hardest task. This acceptance lets us become the living light in our own lives. When we surrender to the lost and fragmented parts of ourselves and love, adore and cherish ourselves we embody the Guru. This is how we heal ourselves and become whole again.

To own your Guru archetype it is necessary to let go of everything that isn't your self, and be willing to purify your spirit with love and acceptance. You don't need to sit at a Guru's feet to learn to love and care for yourself and direct your life in the path of your heart's desire. To become enlightened and aware of who you are requires letting go of all the delusions of selfhood you have ever ingested from your external world. It means, as well, that you go inside to experience your own wonder and delight. It can help to have the guidance and direction of a loving being to help you when you are stuck with false identifications of yourself. Someone who has had a direct experience of self will always encourage you to find and live from your true self. Whenever you are stuck or blocked it can be useful to seek help from someone who lives their life from this place of love and peace.

Enlightenment has come to many people who live a simple and tranquil life, doing the best they can for themselves and others. These people are not great stars illuminating the minds of the masses. They often live quite content lives and know the Source lives within them and illuminates every aspect of their being. They are a real pleasure and delight to know and to be around.

To own your own God nature requires you to truly want to experience who you are. It is also essential to give up any identifications which limit your beauty, intelligence and wisdom so that you can fully experience in your heart that you are a radiant being, one with the Source. There never has been nor will there ever be anyone as unique as you are. When you share this awareness your will and the will of the Divine become one.

## Exercise

1 Sit in silence, quietly breathing in and out. Hold this stillness deep inside of you. As you let go of the thoughts and pictures in your mind let your identifications of yourself slip away as you begin to enter a state where you are one with your self. You will feel in the depths of your heart that you are connected and have always been one with your self.

2 Ask yourself what is outside of you? Is there anything which is separate from you? If it appears to be can you see that this comes from the dictates of your mind which create the illusion of separation? You may experience everything as separate from you. This is your mind holding sway over you. When you can drop your mind you will experience that you are at one with all life; you are connected. This makes it easy to drop your competitiveness and striving and let yourself rest in the knowledge that you and God are one. This is called surrender. You may find that when you compete you are really only competing with yourself. When you abuse yourself or treat yourself badly you are damaging your vital connection to your self. When you love and honor yourself your worth shines like bright diamonds in the light.

3 Find time every day to be with your self. Find a quiet place where you will not be interrupted and let yourself sit in silent meditation. Let yourself be and know that in the core of your being you are peace, joy and beauty itself. This is the foundation of who you are. The awareness of this will give you the energy, clarity and vitality you will need for your daily life.

## The Myth Of The Guru Archetype

The myth that we are separate from the Source feeds our fears that we are nothing on our own or that we need to do something to be blessed or rewarded by God. We have created that awareness as separate from ourselves. We are, in truth, so glorious that if our light were to fully shine we would be dazzled by the intensity of our own self.

Release anything in your past which binds your attachment to negative ideas you have about who you think you are. Forgive all those who need forgiving and move into the light of the self. Here you will find joy and strength. This is the center where all is serene, beautiful and peaceful. Enjoy it.

The myth that there are people who are more evolved than we are or who have answers which we need is prevalent in spiritual communities throughout the world. What a Guru truly gives you is the opportunity to experience your self. It cannot give you any answers which are outside of you. If you allow yourself to be at one with life and to recognize that you are all knowing and all loving then you will be aware that everything you need already exists within you.

What you may have to do to reach this level of clarity and awareness requires patience and real work on yourself. If you follow the path of spiritual development you will know that the truly great teachers can only offer you an experience of self. There is absolutely nothing else to give. That experience of yourself is all that you could possibly need. Anyone who pretends to have answers that you don't have or requires you to serve them in some way is only taking your spiritual freedom from you. The truly great teachers ask only that you be yourself and respect and honor yourself deeply. They create the space and the atmosphere for this to happen.

True spiritual awakening is not an external manifestation, it is an act of releasing the mind of all negativity and letting the beauty and grace of the spirit shine. It is simple and doesn't require you to be any other way than how you are. From this you learn to trust that who you are is perfectly acceptable and lovely. Remember you are always free to choose your path. You are the Guru any time you choose to be that who you are, your self.

# MEDITATION

Sit in a comfortable and relaxed position with your spine straight and let your breathing be soft and rhythmical. Allow yourself to come back to your Self. Feel your eyes pulling back towards the back of your head and feel your Crown chakra opening at the top of your head.

Imagine golden light coming in through the crown of your head. This light floods through your body starting at the top of your head and moving down through each chakra. It moves down through your Crown and Brow chakra and into your Throat chakra, filling your lungs and expanding into your Heart chakra. It fills your back and shoulders and moves down your arms and into your hands. This light now moves further into your body to the Solar Plexus, removing toxins and waste as it moves down into your lower back and the Sacral chakra.

Here it cleanses your liver and stomach, your digestive organs and your kidneys, as it moves into your bowels and genital organs. It moves on into your Root chakra and then down your legs and into your feet and toes.

Feel the light cleansing your entire body and your energy system. It moves through you and connects you with the earth. This light soothes you and takes away any pain or stress. This light is love and is a gift from your self to you. It comforts you and brings you peace. When you acknowledge the Source with thanks and gratitude for your ever deepening awareness of self you can rest in the peace of your own light.

It is enough to say "Thank you for who I am" and come back to your normal waking consciousness.

## Vitality

The kind of energy this archetype brings is a different type of vitality from the kind you need for playing a game of tennis. It is a form of energy which is so refined and sensitive that jarring movements or fractious behavior can unsettle it. It is, in fact, still, yet flowing.

This energy can give you the stamina and vitality to withstand highly stressful or difficult situations. It can fortify you during crisis and stress and it can open you to joy and beauty as well. This energy is the special vitality required of people who do demanding tasks and never seem to tire.

This is the energy of the spirit and it works on an inner plane when we cultivate awareness with love and harmony. People who have achieved this archetype have an unusual kind of stamina and vitality. They often do what would appear to normal eyes to be extraordinary feats, requiring tremendous vitality and energy. They are channeling energy from the Higher Self to accomplish whatever is asked of them.

This is also the energy we use when we are being creative. When we open to the Source we become co-creators of the universe and in turn, of our own lives. At this level whatever we consciously imagine has the potential to manifest into reality. Our spirits are creative and whatever we do with our creativity helps to refine our spiritual energy for healing and transformation. Allow yourself to open to this place within and experience its beauty and serenity.

To channel the vitality from the Guru archetype, you can do the following.

Practice meditation for 15–20 minutes daily

Reflect on the nature of your true self

Pray for peace and well-being for yourself and all sentient beings

Laugh with others and share your joy

Develop compassion for all life

Read books by the world's spiritual leaders

## Empowerment

When we acknowledge the Guru archetype within ourselves we are reconnecting to the highest and most refined energy available to us.

We are uniting our consciousness with the eternal and sacred within our spirit. As we empower ourselves in the fullest way we honor our Divine essence.

*I am one with the Source.*

*I am the truth, the light and the way.*

*I am united with all souls throughout eternity.*

*My power rests in being who I am.*

*I am love. I am joy. I am freedom.*

*I am peace and serenity.*

*Who I am is me.*

*There is no separation. I am one with all life.*

*I thank the Source for the profound experience of myself.*

*Gratitude awakens the good to unfold in my life.*

*I acknowledge that all my past experiences have brought me to this moment of love and total acceptance.*

*I create my life consciously and with love.*

*I channel my highest good and greatest joy to renew and transform my life.*

# CONCLUSION

We all need awareness, vitality and empowerment for living happy lives. We want to be loved, accepted and respected and it is sometimes difficult to realize that we must give ourselves these things before anyone else can give them to us. It may take us a lifetime to come to grips with our talents and gifts. No one ever said it would be easy and only we can decide that who we are and what we have to offer the world is worth the struggle and pain of putting our light forward. It can be lonely and frightening and we may feel that we are doing the wrong thing at times. However, it can also be fun, challenging and rewarding when we allow our potential to manifest and we witness the directions becoming clearer about what we should do for ourselves and where we need to go to do that. We have the opportunity of meeting some wonderful people along the path of light, as well as the opportunity of sharing some deeply beautiful moments where we feel absolutely connected and one with life and the world around us. These experiences make the journey worthwhile.

Whatever you decide to do for your development and growth, the prayer is to do it with love. Life will present you with all the challenges you need for your growth. When you have met them to the best of your ability, don't stay stuck in them, move onto higher levels of awareness and light. Trust the Source within you to guide and protect you. You are never alone. The light of your Divine Nature will always draw to you the friends and teachers you need. We are all students and we are all learning. Eventually you'll understand that growing is the ultimate challenge in life.

May you be blessed with good fortune in your quest. God bless us all.

# RELATED BOOKS BY CROSSING PRESS

### All Women Are Healers: A Comprehensive Guide to Natural Healing
*By Diane Stein*
A wealth of information on various healing methods including Reiki, reflexology, polarity balancing, and homeopathy, intended to help women take control of their bodies and lives.
Paper • ISBN-13: 978-0-89594-409-2 / ISBN-10: 0-89594-409-X

### Color and Crystals: A Journey Through the Chakras
*By Joy Gardner Gordon*
Healing with stones, color, and tarot archetypes.
Paper • ISBN-13: 978-0-89594-258-6 / ISBN-10: 0-89594-258-5

### The Healing Energy of Your Hands
*By Michael Bradford*
"Anyone who has come into contact with Michael Bradford knows that he channels spiritual energy with the focus of a laser beam. This energy leaps out of his book to enlighten us all."
—Lewis Walker, M.D.

Paper • ISBN-13: 978-0-89594-781-9 / ISBN-10: 0-89594-781-1

### Healing with the Energy of the Chakras
*By Ambika Wauters*
Wauters presents a self-help program giving you guidelines and a framework within which to explore and understand how your energetic system responds to thoughts and expression. This can help you shift your perceptions about who you are and what life can offer you.
Paper • ISBN-13: 978-0-89594-906-6 / ISBN-10: 0-89594-906-7

### Homeopathic Color Remedies
*By Ambika Wauters*
Light and color are powerful in providing a source of healing. Color relationships to specific chakras play an important part in rebalancing and realigning our energy. Wauters' homeopathic color remedies serve as medicine for our energy body, increasing the energetic flow physically, emotionally, and mentally
Paper • ISBN-13: 978-0-89594-997-4 / ISBN-10: 0-89594-997-0

### Life Changes with the Energy of the Chakras
*By Ambika Wauters*
When we face up to the reality of change, we learn to accept its challenges with grace and renewed grit. In this book Ambika Wauters will help you open that closed door, so that you can get to the place of healing.
Paper • ISBN-13: 978-1-58091-020-0 / ISBN-10: 1-58091-020-3

# RELATED BOOKS BY CROSSING PRESS

**The Sevenfold Journey**
**Reclaiming Mind, Body & Spirit Through the Chakras**
*By Anodea Judith & Selene Vega*
Combining yoga, movement, psychotherapy, and ritual, the authors weave ancient and modern wisdom into a powerful tapestry of techniques for facilitating personal growth and healing.
Paper • ISBN-13: 978-0-89594-574-7 / ISBN-10: 0-89594-574-6

**We are the Angels**
**Healing Your Past, Present, and Future with the Lords of Karma**
*By Diane Stein*
Explores the possibilities for healing our energy, ourselves, and our planet. Based on the premise that the Earth and all beings are one, Stein masterfully presents a detailed understanding of karma—the accrued lessons of past lifetimes continuing in the present—and the process of healing and releasing karmic patterns and situations.
Paper • ISBN-13: 978-0-89594-878-6 / ISBN 0-89594-878-8

For a current catalog of books from Crossing Press,
visit our Web site at: **www.tenspeed.com**